# Master Your Dream Job:

*And Find A Job You Love, Career,
Creative Business, Discover Your Inner
Voice; New Skills, Talents, or Fresh
New Ideas.*

**By Leon Lyons**

# Table of Contents

# Chapter 1: How to find a perfect job

*"Your work is to discover your work and then with all your heart to give yourself to it."* —
**Buddha**

Do you dream of having a perfect job? Do you occasionally spend time considering a future where you are paid to do what you love? Wouldn't it be a dream come true if you could get your ideal job doing something that you are good at? It would be the ultimate realisation of any underpaid, overworked, unappreciated employee. Even if you are already employed and the pay is good enough, it's always better to get paid doing something you love rather than working at a job you don't care about. But these circumstances could not be described as ideal or perfect.

It is easier to talk about your ideal life than actually going to find your perfect job, career and life; but it can be achieved with strong commitment, concentration, and determination. Your return investment should far outweigh the effort that you put into your job.

What would you give in order for your work, career, and life to be perfect?

Those who feel their jobs and careers are perfect are the happiest and feel the most fulfilled. That doesn't mean that your version of a perfect life needs to be exactly the same as others. Perfection is a unique trait. Anyone willing to make an effort to define, discover, and pursue perfection can also achieve it.

What does a perfect life look like for you? It does not need to be what your family and friends define as perfection, but rather the perfection that you have designated for yourself.

We tend to look at what we have and wonder, "Would I be happier elsewhere? Did I choose the right career? Do I have to look for another job in order to get a better wage?" All these factors come into play and cause us to question our decision to take on a new job, join a new company, or remain where we are.

Is there a perfect job for you out there? This feeling is subjective and uncertain, but there are clear signs that you may have found the perfect job! Let's take a closer look at what this may feel like.

## 1.1 What is a perfect job

There are many concepts and definitions of what a perfect job should look like. For some, it might be the one that takes little-to-no commuting, whereas many would be willing to commute for a higher-paying job.

In a perfect world, we would find an ideal job the very first time we went in search of it. However, finding a career that brings you happiness, a sense of accomplishment, and interpersonal relationships that you enjoy will take a lot of trial and error. The trick is to precisely define what you want and never give up on finding it until it's yours.

We all want to find a fun and meaningful dream job, but what does that mean?
Many people think the answer includes finding their dream jobs through a flash of insight, while others believe the key elements are that it's simple and highly paid.

There are many qualities of an ideal job. But in fact, there never exists an ideal job at all. Nonetheless, one would expect an ideal job or a perfect job to be work that has the following characteristics:

- You continuously succeed (Growth Opportunity & Salary).
- You have the aptitude for your job duties.
- There are colleagues that you enjoy working with.

- There is a great environment that provides you with exceptional growth opportunities, irrespective of whether you have joined at a lower or middle level.
- You have respect for the management you are working with.

Some employers offer a standardised career growth plan, as in the case of government employment, while others have incentives for out-of-turn growth as a performance incentive. Small, active businesses will not have too many organisational ranks, unlike large corporations.

**Ideal Career Must Have #1 - Adequate Pay**
This may as well be at the top of the list. A car, benefits, or paid vacation may be included in your payment plan. Until accepting an offer, you can compare salaries for your career level across the industry.

**Ideal Career Must Have #2 - A Good Boss**.
Some people believe it's the boss who makes your career miserable. Whether there is truth to this or not, having a great boss can boost your job experience. Just as companies like to say that excellent employees are hard to find, finding a good boss is just as hard!

If you work for a boss from hell and with co-workers that you hate, you will be unhappy.

Typically, when looking for our dream job, we concentrate solely on the job description and its requirements. But it is just as critical to consider who you will be working with. A bad boss can ruin your dream job, but if you can potentially make friends, they can help make a dull job more enjoyable. Not only that - but having a positive workplace culture makes it easy to get help, receive useful feedback, and work together to make everything better.

**Ideal Career Must Have #3 - Great Job Duties**.
Taking on some extra responsibilities at work is another key to your success. Any additional duties you are willing to do can help you step up the ladder. Don't feel obligated to take on too many extra tasks where it conflicts with your primary duty, but understand that you'll at least have to put in a little extra effort in every task that you accomplish.

It's not your salary, status, or the form of business that matters, but what you do every day, hour-by-hour. Employment should be work that draws you in, holds your attention, and gives you a sense of accomplishment. This is why an hour of editing a spreadsheet may feel like pure drudgery, while an hour of playing a computer game may feel like no time at all.

What's the difference between enjoyable and unenjoyable job duties? Why might computer games be engaging while being an office administrator is not? If a job – no matter the type – has the following characteristics, it can be engaging:

1. The right to decide how to do your job
2. Simple activities with a clearly defined beginning and end
3. Variety of job styles
4. Positive feedback is provided so you know when you're doing well

**Ideal Career Must Have #4- Great Working Environment**

An ideal job must have a positive, relaxed working environment that will help you perform your best. There are many situations that can feel unmotivating. But before you start to complain, first look inside yourself. You can fix many workplace issues on your own or with a little help.

You are more likely to be placed in a position that complements your personality if you effectively communicate with your recruiting consultant. An ideal working environment matches the job requirements with an applicant's personality traits to decide if a job is right for them.

You have to have meaningful intentions when finding your ideal job. One day you might find a career that pays so exceptionally well that you can find meaning and purpose for your life outside of the work. Nevertheless, being affluent enough to find meaning away from work does not mean you have found your perfect career.

If the criteria previously described defines perfection, how many of us can say that we already have "the ideal job?" When you imagine what you need to do in order to get your dream job, does it mean that you require each of the qualities mentioned above for a perfect working environment? Most importantly, do you think it's possible to land a job that meets most of the criteria even if you aren't doing what you love?

The theory is to recognise your most significant interest – your passion – and pursue a career involving that interest. "Stick to your passion, and you're going to have a great career," is certainly an enticing message. If we look closely at successful people, we see that they are really passionate and enthusiastic about what they do.

Most successful people are passionate, but their passion has often grown with their successes. Many have taken a long time to discover their passion instead of going with their first obsession. Steve Jobs began with a passion for

Zen Buddhism. As a way to earn some easy and quick money, he got into technology. But as he succeeded, his love for technology grew until he became the most famous advocate for doing what you love.

## 1.2 Finding your Passion

Remember when you were a child? You'd try things without putting any extra thought into it. You never overanalysed the advantages of learning baseball versus football, you would just do it. You would run around the fields playing baseball and soccer. You created sandcastles, played games, asked stupid questions, looked for bugs, dug in the dirt, and pretended to be a sewer monster. No one told you to do it, you just did it. Only your curiosity and enthusiasm led you.

And the beautiful thing was, if you discovered you hated baseball, you just stopped playing it. There was no presence of remorse or regret. There was no inner-debate or argument. You either enjoyed it or you didn't. It was as simple as that.

A well-used expression is to "follow your passion." But if you don't know what your passion is, then what do you do? This is not just a problem for those starting their careers; it can also be an issue for those who feel stuck in jobs that they do not enjoy. To slip into a routine that leaves you bored or unfulfilled is all too easy: you want to make the switch, but you don't know what to do or how to do it. It can be so frustrating to hear people tell you, "Just pursue your heart!" Sure, if only you knew what your passion was, you would follow it.

You are probably the kind of person who works hard, is committed, and diligent. Nothing will deter you if you know what you're doing. If you were only allowed to do one thing to change your life, consider doing something you're passionate about and doing it for the rest of your life.

Okay, it's not as easy as it sounds, but the effort is worth it.
It doesn't necessarily mean you must quit your job or leave your family to pursue your passion. You don't need to do anything drastic. It means you should analyse what you have and start to listen to your gut. It simply means to be grateful for what you have but to follow your heart's nudges as well.

So, what are you going to do? How will you discover your life's passion? Here are some suggestions:

**1.** Ask yourself these two simple questions. You will figure out what to do with the rest of your life by answering these questions frankly.

1) What subject can I read or study about for hours without getting bored?

2) If I had the total financial wealth to do anything, what would I spend my time doing?

**2.** Hunter S. Thompson, the journalist and novelist, once said: "Anything that gets your blood pumping is probably worth it." A lot of things that make you happy are never going to help you earn money. You don't have to be amazing at something to be enthusiastic about it. If you can't imagine a life where you are unable to do that "thing" you love, then that "thing" is your passion. There's no need for it to be a money-maker.

**3.** Think of all the things you hate doing and list the occupations or activities you loathe. Once you have removed these choices, your true passion may become more apparent. You may even want to make a list of people you are jealous of to get more clarification on the topic. Who do you envy? List multiple people, examine the reasons that you envy them, identify what they are doing differently, and try some of those things.

**4.** Find things that you are good at. Even if you don't have exceptional skills at all, most people have lots of specialties they're "okay" at. You might be a fantastic cartoon artist but not good with computers.

"The most successful people are those who are most passionate about their work and not characterized by a unique ability, said Hunter S. Thompson, journalist and novelist. "It's a fusion of talents, often not even exceptional, but they've made their fusion exceptional," he says. Thompson further added, "Steve Jobs wasn't the greatest inventor, entrepreneur, designer, or businessman in the world, but he was uniquely good enough in all these things and fused them into something much greater."

Don't wait for an inspirational Eureka moment that some people are lucky to have, where they immediately know what to do with their lives. Sure, those moments are inspirational, but you cannot wait in vain for such a moment. Your true passion is not instantly known but is learned through a series of discoveries of small interests.

You can have someone close to you help explore your true passion by thinking and analysing the phase of your mind. Try asking close friends and family what they think you should do with your future. But don't just drop everything and do what people suggest without careful consideration, as their suggestions may have been rushed. If any of your nearest and dearest friends have hobbies that spark your interest, ask to spend some time helping them out and/or try them yourself. Experiment with new experiences as much as possible, whether it's a new sport, learning a new language, or practising a craft.

**5.** Recall what you used to do as a kid. Did you love to paint or write stories? Try to remember the things you enjoyed during your youth, before beginning to stress over learning the right subjects or getting a good job. What did you want to do before life got in the way? Would you like to enjoy these things now? To help you discover your true passion as a grownup, use these memories. Maybe you have some hobbies now. Could you build on them and bring them to take more of your life's centre stage?

Or, take a look into your future: imagine you're beyond the age of retirement. Would you be proud of what you've been doing for the last 20 or 30 years? Think of it as a way of writing your obituary – where your proudest accomplishments are listed. What would like to see for yourself?

**6.** Create something brand new. Creating something new is the secret to discovering your passion. People who start from scratch are immediately excited about projects, start-up companies, or new services they offer. You can design new cushions, write stories of your favourite genre, or launch a Twitter account dedicated to fact-checking politicians. You've got to find success to fuel your passion.

**7.** Imagine getting up early, leaping out of bed, and feeling excited to go to work. You get dressed quickly, full of enthusiasm for your day. The sun shines, and you're taking the first steps out of your apartment. Now imagine where you're going and what kind of work you will be doing based on that sense of anticipation. You might put in more hours than the average person, but it's okay because your working hours are just zooming by. Often you are in a state of mind, sometimes called a "flow," where you lose track of the world and the time, losing yourself in the task at hand. Employment to you is not the same as it is referred to by many people, but actually something enjoyable, exciting, and fun. It's a passion rather than "a job." This may sound like a pipe dream to you if you have a career you despise or even hate. If you don't try to find out what you're curious about, you're right: there's never going to be positive change. Dare to dream, dare to imagine the possibilities, and dare to search for what you love. It's not just an opportunity to change your life.

What if you went to a restaurant with a strong, negative opinion? "I'm not hungry. I don't want to eat anything here. I don't even want to be here." Well, if you look at it that way, the menu won't look appealing. You're not going to explore it with proper time or attention, and you're unlikely to find food that you will enjoy eating. The same principle applies to the

14

hunt for a job that you love. If you're sure it will be hard to find your passion, or that it just won't happen for you, you're going to remain closed to all the possibilities. You're going to block the little nudges, pulls, and signals that lead us all where we need to be. After all, if you don't believe it exists, how can you expect to find fulfilling work?

Once you decide that you want to discover your passion, get out your metal detector; it's time to look for signs of what you're fond of doing. When you check your life's environment, you can find some peak encounters. Diving into these "peak times" and finding the key ingredients is really important.

Look for the over-arching umbrella. When you look at all the ingredients that are important to you, they may seem entirely disconnected at first. Let's say you love French, you drink coffee, you like to interpret and categorise, and you're a community leader. How can you build a career out of these passions? It would be like peering into your cupboard and seeing cocoa powder, tofu, and carrots and wondering: how can I make anything delicious with these ingredients?

Make sure you know the difference between a hobby and a profitable love. You can fall head-over-heels in love with an experience that engrosses you— something that lights you up and makes your heart sing. But now you have to ask yourself the next question: Who would benefit from my hobby, and who will pay for it?

If you want to contribute your passion to society and make a profit from it, you need to be rational as to whether it could turn into a career, and if so, what you need to do to make it happen. Additionally, think about if you'd even like doing those things as a job; for some people, a passion is just fun, and turning it into work turns it from "I love doing this" into a "I have to do this."

We all have a lot of fears that talk to us in soft voices, telling us not to do what we love. These fears could be about the possibility of failure, poor performance, exposure, and vulnerability. If you let those voices prevail, they will push your passion out of your reach – don't let that negative inner-voice win. Just give your best shot with all the available resources, and things will start coming into place. This doesn't mean that you should be reckless or act in haste, but rather make every decision a wise one, calculate your moves, and stay optimistic.

People might call you bold, irresponsible or courageous, but rather than interpreting that as meaning you are too risky, you need to see it in a more positive light. Just look at it more as being committed to your happiness and freedom rather than being comfortable with the status quo. Find a courageous version of yourself. Figure out what threats you're facing. The road to passion is where you do things that scare you without leaving you in a constant state of fear. Broaden your comfort zone.

Get out a sheet of paper, brainstorm, and jot down any job ideas that come to mind right away. Everything that comes to your mind, simply write it down. You might find inspirations in your house, on your tablet, or your bookshelf. At this point, there are no terrible ideas. Write it down on paper and think about your options later.

It is best to stay in your current career while exploring your possibilities. So, with that being said, don't just quit your job. Don't give up and resign tomorrow if you decide on your dream job or your passion. It's best if you can do your passion as a side job and build up profits for a couple of months or a year. It allows you to build up some money (and if you go into business on your own, you will need that cash reserve) while learning the skills you need.

Try your idea first before you leap into it as a career. Do it as a hobby or a side job at first so you can see if it's your true calling. You may be excited about it for a couple of days, but will you be enthusiastic about it for at least a few months? If you pass this test and find you still love doing it, you've probably found the perfect job for you.

Explore your passion as much as possible. If this has been a hobby for a while, you may already have a solid foundation. Continue to learn - read every article on the topic and buy the best books available. Do not go into this as a new career with only a novice skill level - learn and practice some more. You need to have professional skills if you want to make money. Become an expert.

Find other people who are doing what you want to do for a living, either on the field or on the internet, and ask them about their work. LinkedIn is a great place to start. Once you find a person you would like to connect with, ask them questions such as:

- What exactly are you doing in your job?
- What kind of education and training did you need?
- Which skills do you find absolutely necessary?

- How did you get started in this field?
- What are your recommendations for me?

You will often find that individuals who love their jobs are more than willing to give advice free of charge.

## 1.3 Evaluating your passion

When evaluating your passion, you must know your own expectations. What makes you enthusiastic or motivates you? Is your passion sustainable? More often than not, your aspirations are out of sync with reality.

Sometimes, you might even feel there is nothing you are passionate about. You might be interested in things, but not truly passionate about them. If you don't think you are passionate about anything, at least continue with what you're interested in. For once in your life, let yourself have fun and do what you want to do. That doesn't mean you've got to quit your job. You can explore your passions on the side and see where they can take you.

If people say, "I don't know where to start," it actually means, "I don't know what direction to take in order to succeed." They're unsure about how to get to their final destination. Consider taking tiny steps if you know what you are interested in. Forget about the consequences of the small steps. We were always taught to do something big, but forget about it! Think small.

Eliminate the pressure you have put on yourself. Pressure and stress are unnecessary and rarely serve any benefits. There's no rush. You can't control the outcome. You're going to end up exhausting yourself if you try. You don't have to pursue your passion, but it is something you should at least discover.

Excuses, doubts and concerns are simply beliefs that can stop you from living the reality you desire. Having those thoughts does not mean that you can't do anything. Simply use the power of thought to stop yourself from thinking negatively. The problem isn't your ability to learn; the problem is actually your negative thoughts. You must let them pass by. Think of these thoughts like a radio. It's currently playing a song that you loathe. But if you leave it alone, a new song will come on without you messing with it. If you become fixated on your negative thoughts or your "can't do" attitude, you will veer off your path towards what you want.

Staying relaxed throughout the process is very important. Because during the process, your mind is bubbling with new thoughts. New thoughts and new possibilities will constantly emerge.

**Here are seven tips on how to cultivate your passions and make them concrete.**

1. **Find Your Passions**

   It makes sense that you must first find your passions before you can expand and master them. What would you like to do? What do you dream of doing? Have you got a favourite pastime (maybe more than one) that you can transform into a dream job? If you are not sure about what you want, or maybe have varied interests in multiple areas, consider taking an aptitude test.

2. **Create Your Passion**

   When your passion has been established, spend some time cultivating it. If you're excited about a particular thing, focus on it. Practise! Write to a newspaper. Join a group of artists. You should network. Make friends read your work and criticise it. If you enjoy photography, go out and take some pictures! Take pictures of all kinds— close-ups and landscape photos, portraits, and significant events. Invest in a decent camera and learn how to use it.

Whatever your passion is, pursue it. Your vision may require a college education, so look for options in your area of interest and start a degree program. Alternatively, you might find that shorter programs or courses will suffice.

## 3. Set Specific Goals

Set specific goals to grow your passion. Many of us make lists every day, but that's not enough. For each day you may have specific steps, but also think about what you want to do by the end of the week, the month, and a year from now. Then set goals for those dreams to be accomplished. Set goals to learn how to set up your website— and work on it if you're an aspiring blogger. Aim to submit an article to a magazine editor. Set your deadlines, and you'll be more likely to reach them.

## 4. Find Accountability

Now that you have set your goals, find someone to hold you accountable. In addition to teaching you what you need to learn to get going in your profession, a mentor or coach can also be the one to check in to see how far you have come in achieving your goals. A mentor can ask thought-provoking questions to help you identify where you want your long-term life and career to go, and what you need to do to get there. Also, a mentor can help you define success — the kind that goes beyond what your employer or industry defines as success. People with similar interests can also surround you. A writing group is great for authors. If you are seeking an education in the same major or degree program, you will undoubtedly find ways to get together with others. Keep track of each other. Encourage each other.

## 5. Take Breaks

If you're excited about achieving your goals, you may find it difficult to find time to relax. It might feel hard to connect with family and friends on time. To prevent this, it is essential to take breaks and be with those you care for. Keep up with what's necessary for your personal life. Your target is not going anywhere. Once you get there, it will be so much sweeter to share your success with your loved ones.

## 6. Re-evaluate your progress

At some point, sit back and think about where you are and what progress you've made. It may be too early to re-evaluate after one month, so shoot for three months and then six months. Look at your targets and compare them to your current path. If all of these goals are achieved along the way, then congratulate yourself. If you don't achieve your goals, then you must re-evaluate your plan. Did you work hard enough? Do you have to do something differently? Or were your goals too high to begin with? In this phase, be rational as you take steps to achieve your goals, and you will be more likely to stick to your target with each step.

## 7. Keep Developing Your Passion

Once you have found your passion, you feel it's definitely your dream career, and you have achieved some level of success, it's time to enjoy it. BUT, never be lazy about it! Take a class or attend a conference to learn the latest developments in your profession. Conferences are perfect for networking with others who have common interests of their own. Connecting with these people will give you new information and maybe a renewed enthusiasm for what you do.

Being passionate about a job is more about your heart than it is about your brain. This is important because it takes a mixture of your heart and head to achieve your full potential. Your intellectual ability and expertise will only carry you so far.

You'll have tough days, months, and years, regardless of your talent. With a crappy boss, you might feel trapped. You may be discouraged, and you may want to give up. What's getting you through these tough times? Your enthusiasm: it is the vital rocket fuel that helps you overcome challenges and succeed even in dark times. Passion is the product of a belief in a cause or the joy of doing the activities that you love. It encourages you to stay on the path to develop your skills, overcome adversity, and find meaning in your work and life.

Using mental models is another way to help you learn about your needs and interests. Pose a question, then say what you're going to do — and why. Here are some examples of these models:

> • If you had only one year left to live, how would you spend it? What does that teach you about what you're doing and what you're passionate about?

- If you knew that you would be very successful in your career, what job would you do today?
- What do you want to tell your kids and grandchildren about your career accomplishments? How are you going to explain what profession you have chosen?
- What would you say about a career choice if you were a third-party advising yourself?

To meet your potential, enthusiasm is essential. You are getting in touch with your passions that allow you to concentrate more on your hopes and dreams along with your fears and insecurities. You don't have to know immediately what to do or determine if your dream is even possible. In this endeavour, there is an aspect of brainstorming - you don't want to destroy ideas until you examine them. Again, let's focus on what's going on before you worry about how you can reach your goals. First and foremost, these activities are about self-awareness. Consider how much more likely you are to find openings if you are aware of what you are looking for.

## 1.4 Working Towards Goals

Big and small goals can be your path to a better life, and the way you set them can make a difference.

Having aspirations for what we want to do and working towards our goals is a vital part of being human. The road to our goals may not always be smooth or straightforward, but having them is part of what makes life enjoyable. They provide us with a sense of purpose and meaning, lead us in the directions we want to go, and keep us excited and motivated - all good things for our overall happiness.

Aristotle said more than 2000 years ago, "Well begun is half done." And in terms of goals, he's right (as he seems to have been right on several other things). Focusing on how we set our goals makes us more likely to reach them and makes us think positively about ourselves and our lives.

It's easy to set goals, but it's hard to work towards them, change your life, and start new habits. You might still have a very long way to go towards achieving your goal. Or, it might be hard doing something every single day, long after the sparkle of starting something new wears off. It can be difficult, but making your plans of self-improvement public to your peers and the world is one of the best ways to hold yourself accountable, turn thoughts into goals, and behaviours into lifestyles.

If you follow these rules, you will have a much higher chance to achieve the goals you set.

**Create a List**
If you've got the time right now, you could run off a list of things you've always wanted to do. If you can create a list, that means you've got goals even if you don't have the time or energy to work on them right now. The feeling is also natural— we all want to have extra time in our day. The key to overcoming procrastination is to find a way to get you started on your goals, and let the momentum take you where you need to be.

An essential part of achieving your goal is to find the inspiration you need to get you going. Inspiration is more important than the method you're using, more important than writing it down, and more important than the next obstacles you might face. The obstacles are coming, and that's why you are going to have to feel ready to have your friends, family, and the general public watching you as you work towards your goals.

## Narrow Down your List

When we sit down to think about what we want to accomplish; we often start a list and start writing down all the things we want. And really, it's a great way to start. The problem is that we often end up with a long list of things that we want to accomplish, and it becomes tough to decide which goals are essential and which are less critical. Alternatively, set some parameters once you've written your list. Perhaps you only give yourself five goals a year, for starters. This means that for two months, you can provide total focus on each individual target.

## Write your Goals Down

Write your goals down carefully. Write down how you're going to know that you've accomplished your goals and by when you'd like to do it. Ask yourself: what's it going to look like, and how am I going to feel when I complete it? Describe your goal in specific terms and dates, e.g., "By the end of May, I want to plant lettuces, carrots, and peas in the empty spot in my garden," rather than "I want to do some planting." Write down your goals in terms of what you want, not what you don't want. For example: "I want to be able to wear my beloved jeans again, instead of, "I no longer want to be overweight." Say your goals out loud to somebody. It seems to increase the likelihood that we will stick to them by telling everyone we know about our goals.

By allowing yourself to focus on just one goal for two months, you'll have a much better chance of making it a true habit than if you're trying to change several practises at once. Once you've met your first goal, it'll be high time to hop on to your next target until your pattern improves, and it becomes normal for you.

Once you have selected your five goals or targets, find a connection that they have. There will often be a clear link between the goals. For example, two of your goals may be to lose weight and get in shape. These are two targets that go together, of course, so you can plan to work on these goals simultaneously.

**Have a Good Reason as to "Why" You Want to Reach a Goal**
A purpose-free goal is an unfortunate target. You need to know why you must achieve that objective. Your "why" is personal and can often be quite embarrassing if you explain it to someone else. An essential part is that it needs to be YOUR reason why you want to achieve your goal, not because someone else says it's a good idea.

If you're a smoker who is consulting with a doctor, your doctor would probably say that you should give up smoking for your long-term health. But that's not YOUR "why." You might enjoy smoking and not be concerned about the long-term effects, in which case your "why" is uncertain.

The same goes for weight loss. You might be perfectly happy with your weight as it is. If someone says you should lose weight, that's not your "why." Your "why" must be personal and have some sort of emotional connection with what you want. "I want to lose weight" is an excellent personal reason to set your goal for your well-being.

It's up to you. Talk about something you'd like to do or a place you'd like to work for. As long as you want to do it, it doesn't concern anyone else. It should be something that you want to do, not what someone else expects you to do. It's for your own sake.

### Set Weekly Objectives
Some goals need to be broken down into steps, or objectives. They can be huge objectives, or just little ones. It might be easier to work on something simple in order to get you moving at times. And if your overall goal is just a little bit beyond what you can handle right now, it often

helps to meet the smaller objectives to keep you motivated.

Staying focused on objectives is one of the hardest parts of achieving goals, but breaking them down into bite-size goals like this helps you stay focused on the process. After you plan what you want to accomplish and feel motivated and determined, you will undoubtedly continue to face the daily crisis and problems that are thrown at us. It can be frustrating to remain focused on your goals when that happens. Spend some time each week to resolve this and set one or two goals that will get you closer to achieving your target.

For example, if your goal is to save $20,000 next year, you'll need to change your spending habits now. So, if you're used to shopping every weekend or spending an excessive amount of time looking for the new digital gadget on Amazon, you're going to have to stop doing that! Set an objective to either decrease your Amazon shopping by a specified amount or eliminate that habit completely. Alternatively, get to know your savings account. Develop the habit of sending money to your savings account instead of right to Amazon. Set the goal of saving $385 that week (or not spending $385 that week).

If you aim to get fit and lose weight, set the number of days you're going to exercise every week and how much weight you're going to lose. Set a smaller target such as "I will run regularly," or even, "I will run around the park for 20 minutes without stopping."

**Prepare Your First Move**

An ancient Chinese proverb says the "1000-mile journey begins with a single step". Even if your target is not to walk 1000 miles, it will help you to get going by thinking about the first step you will take. Even if you don't know where to begin, there's no excuse. Your first step might be to search "how-to" on the internet, think of people you can consult with, or even get a book from the library on the topic.

Then think about your next step. And your next step. Keep going. It may be frustrating and challenging at times to work towards your goals, so you need to persevere. If a move you're taking isn't working, think of something else that you might try to keep moving you forward, even if it's just a little bit. If you're fighting, ask people you know about what you can do with those thoughts. Thinking of different ways to achieve our goals increases the likelihood that we will succeed. If you're stuck, take a break and then re-read the goal that you wrote down at the start. If your target needs to be changed, that's all right too. Then think of another little next step.

Write down your more modest goals and try to set a few dates as well. Setting multiple, smaller goals makes each one a little easier and gives us a sense of prosperity along the way, which also makes it more likely that we are going to stay on track with our bigger goal.

## Review Your Goals Weekly, Not Daily

Going through your goals every single day and seeing a lack of growth will make you numb. You're just beginning to go through the motions on your list, and if you read it daily, it will quickly stop having any meaningful impact.

Pick a day of the week and schedule some time for contemplation. Reflect on what you've accomplished and how you're doing with your goals that week. Analyse where you're vulnerable, where you've been tempted to stray, and where you've struggled. Make and execute a plan to make sure the same thing doesn't happen the next week and set one or two goals to achieve. Your goals will remain relevant to you this way. Every week, you can give yourself realistic mini goals that will get you closer to your overall goals.

**Celebrate**
Take time to enjoy it when you reach your goal and thank those who have supported you. Think of what you've done along the way and what you have learned.

Now think, what will be your next target or project? Goals are essential in life because they give you a sense of purpose, and a sense of purpose gives you a reason for energy and enthusiasm to wake up in the morning. The purpose is to get you through tough days and contribute to your overall happiness and well-being.

# Chapter 2: Become the Self-Expert

*"They often miss opportunities because they are wrapped in overalls and look like jobs"* –**Thomas A. Edison**

Do you recognise when you are holding yourself back? Are you trying to protect yourself from failure? Most of us live our lives unaware of whether we are on a detrimental or beneficial course, bottling up mistakes and bad decisions so that we don't have to feel the pain of facing them. But this lack of awareness has a noticeable effect on our quality of life.

That's why it is critical to becoming a self-expert. A self-expert is someone who devotes their time to profoundly thinking about their craft. They are dedicated to self-improvement and are willing to look at themselves openly and honestly to make improvements that will improve the quality of their life.

Understanding ourselves is one of the hardest to do. Most of us lack the self-awareness that we need to recognise when we harm ourselves versus helping ourselves to improve. This can have a very detrimental effect on our health and happiness (scratch that - our entire life)!

If we encounter something negative our awareness of how it made us feel is muffled and less perceptible. When we make a mistake, we often ignore it and attempt to unintentionally cover it up without even realising that we're doing it, never having the opportunity to make any real tangible changes.

But how do we become an expert in our own right? What does it take? What are the fundamental principles for cultivating self-expertise? Above all, there is one idea that serves as the very basis for becoming a self-expert. If you can learn this theory, you can become an expert and benefit from better health and happiness in the process.

## 2.1 Finding your strengths, values, and experiences

"What are your strengths?" is a commonly asked question at an interview. It seems straightforward enough, but these four words are presenting candidates with somewhat of a minefield. That's because you have to walk between two directions carefully: too modest on one foot, too brazen on the other. Most candidates do not respond well to that question. Too much modesty and you will undersell your abilities and expertise, causing the boss to conclude that you are less talented than you are. Yet sell too much of yourself, and you can easily find yourself in a team of people that are just as self-interested and potentially unable to function well as a team. If you don't prepare a proper answer to that question, both of these results can happen by accident. You can quickly end up drawing a blank or concentrating too hard on that one strength you can bring if you are caught off guard.

"Out of our weaknesses, our strengths grow." – Ralph Waldo Emerson
Knowing your strengths and weaknesses in your life and career can be of tremendous value. This awareness is invaluable because it helps you focus on the right things in an optimal way. This will also help you make better career decisions and move forward with your life choices.

Understanding your strengths will enable you in tough moments. On the other hand, knowing your vulnerabilities will encourage you to gain the support you need in critical areas where you need the most help. Therefore, by increasing the required support and resources you need to achieve your goal, you can turn these weaknesses into strengths.

You will see the following advantages when you clearly understand your strengths:

- By focusing on things that will earn you the highest returns, you will save money.
- You become more resourceful and make better decisions daily.
- You can raise your expectations and thus increase your performance.
- You will add value to others and the world around you.
- You will naturally improve your self-confidence because there will be more trust in your life all of a sudden.

Understanding your strengths, in general, will allow you to make smarter decisions and choices about your life, career, goals, and other circumstances. For example, you will have more insight into the career path that would best suit your natural talents, trends, and skills. And when it comes to your goals, knowing your strengths will help you set a clear course of action that takes advantage of your muscles, thereby allowing you to make the most of your available time as well as the chances that life throws your way.

You can also reap some benefits as you clearly understand what your limitations are:

- You will focus your time on things that offer you the most confidence and self-assurance.

- You can assign duties and assignments to others who are more likely to accomplish them.
- By concentrating on just the things you are naturally good at, you will dramatically reduce the levels of stress, anxiety, fatigue, and frustration.

When you go through this evaluation process, it's essential to understand your strengths and weaknesses clearly. However, focusing on your muscles will be of the most significant value because that's where your competitive advantage lies after all, and that's where you'll derive the most benefit from your time, energy and effort.

You can find your strengths within the things that look easy for you to learn. Such qualities may also manifest as habits, traits, innate gifts, skills gained, and abilities that you have that you may have looked over. These are subjects of your life that you have built through sustained, concentrated effort. Because you have given so much time working on these areas of your life, you are qualified and able to achieve those tasks and activities at a higher level than most others.

As we come into this world, we naturally develop our interests in life early as a result of very particular experiences in life. These interests influence how we think about these things. As we think about these things, we know more about them; and as we learn more, we know more. As a result, we become more skilled in specific areas of our lives.

Despite having amazing abilities, none of us are born with them. Yes, some of us are likely to have some innate skills, but most of our strengths come from our interests. Our curiosity leads us to such desires, and we may be more interested in some aspects of life. Our curiosity drives us to want to know more about these fields through learning, and as we gain more experience, we begin to develop skills that will take us forward for the rest of our lives.

For example, you may have noticed your parents or peers did things in a certain way when you were young. Such encounters made a lasting impression on your mind because you were so young and impressionable at the time. Although you never personally took part in these tasks or events at the time, as a result of your observations, you gained the requisite knowledge.

Then, you find yourself in a similar situation several years later. Things just happen to come naturally to you without any personal experience. People call you intelligent and tell

41

you that you have natural talent and ability in this area. However, little do they know, you are dominant in this area because of your interests and the sharp observation skills that ignited your curiosity at a young age.

These are the kinds of qualities you need to tap into and use to help move your life further in a more positive way.

Here are five tips to help you determine your strengths at work and adapt them to your job:

**1. Hear what others think you are great at doing.**

What skills do you appreciate? Others might see the qualities that you don't see in yourself. For instance, pay attention and see if you receive positive feedback on your listening skills or your wild imagination. Ask a fellow work friend to spend a couple of minutes talking about what she considers to be your greatest strength. Then ask yourself whether the assumptions are realistic.

Has honesty come up as a strength? Let's say a client's budget is not appropriate for their project goals, and you advise them to take a different route. This consistency with being honest may manifest itself at work as a positive trait. Notice the investment return for your openness (e.g., an increased budget, consumer trust, more projects). Make sure to bring it up in your subsequent analysis of results.

If dedication and reliability emerged as strengths, note occasions that these attributes paid off for your team. Include event preparation in your outline if your organization depends on you to arrange meetings and set up conferences.

## 2. Just do what you're doing.

If you were given the right to do anything you liked for the rest of your working life, what would you choose? This may be a daunting task, but go for it — dream big! Look at the things in and out of work that you like to do. If you enjoy writing but don't get a chance to do a lot at work, consider ways to write to your team in your current position, such as an internal blog or newsletter. If you're an extroverted developer who loves to talk about your work, look for opportunities for technical sales. It is essential to know where your talents and desires lie in designing a career map that plays with your greatest strengths.

### 3. Find your state of flow.

Consider an ordinary workday. What kind of projects do you like to immerse yourself in? Would you prefer uninterrupted work or writing technical specs? What do you do when the hours seem to melt away at your desk?

### 4. Know the style of your relationship.

Knowing what kind of relationships are best for you and what kind of relationships are the toughest for you will help you navigate through the professional waters. If one of your main strengths is to perform drama-free negotiation, ask for opportunities to serve on buying committees or encourage informal mediation among team members who don't see eye-to-eye.

### 5. Maximize the sum of your specialties.

Most job applicants rely on generalisations to find a job, such as being a "people person" or an "organisational wizard." These are great qualities, but if you give specifics, you'll stand out more. Tell employers that you are a "conference planning ninja," or that you can "create project schedules and make detailed predictions like nobody's business." You may have experience working on a marketing team, but you're excited about SEO. This is a unique ability, and you can go a long way if you master it. Maximising your skills not only benefits your career but also makes your team and company more critical.

Generally, when the things you do and the way you do them suit your values, life is good – you're happy and content. But if they don't align with your values, that is when things feel like a burden. This can be a constant source of frustration which is why it is so essential to make a conscious effort to identify your values. There are standards, whether or not you know them. Once you know your values, and when you make plans and choices that uphold them, life can be much more straightforward.

If you love your family but have to work at your job for 70-hour weeks, do you experience internal tension and conflict? And if you don't accept competition, so work in a sales environment is highly competitive, are you going to be satisfied with your job?

Sharing principles can aid in these kinds of situations. You can use them to determine how to live your life because you know your own beliefs, and you can answer questions like this:

- What work should I do?
- Do I have to accept this promotion?
- Do I need to start my own business?
- Should I compromise with my position, or be stubborn with it?
- Do I have to follow the norm or take a new path?

So, take the time to understand the real priorities in your life, and when you identify your values, you will be able to determine the best direction for you and your life goals. Thinking back on your life is an excellent way to start doing this – to recognise when you felt delighted and were genuinely sure that you made good choices.

To get started, here are some more questions:
- What's important to you in life?
- What area of work do you want to improve in this the world?
- What are you most proud of?
- When have you felt the happiest?

Take a sheet of blank paper and get some answers to these questions quickly. Then use these answers as guides to assess your values.

## 2.2 Myers-Briggs Indications can be a Key

The Myers-Briggs Personality Type Indicator is an inventory of self-report designed to identify the type, strengths, and interests of a person's personality. Isabel Myers and her mother, Katherine Briggs, developed the questionnaire based on their experience with Carl Jung's theory of personality styles.

The method of Myers-Briggs defines the personality of an individual by four different aspects of nature, known as dichotomies, preferences, or scales. The first three preferences are based on Jung's writings; Katherine Cook Briggs, based on her own experiences, added the fourth choice, Judging vs. Perceiving.

Depending on the answers to the inventory questions, people are categorised as one of 16 forms of personality. The MBTI is not a "test." Its goal is to enable respondents to explore and further understand their characters - including their likes, dislikes, strengths, weaknesses, potential career preferences, and compatibility with others. No type of personality is "better" or "different" than anyone else. It's not a tool designed to assess mental health or to provide a diagnosis. Instead, its purpose is to help you know more about yourself.

- **Extraversion vs Introversion:**
How is energy gained? Extraverts like being with others and receiving strength from individuals and their environment. Introverts gain power by themselves and require quiet, reflective times throughout the day. The first set of styles is about your energy path. If you choose to focus your energies on dealing with people, events, circumstances, or "the outside world," then Extraversion is your choice. If you prefer to channel your energy to deal with concepts, facts, theories, beliefs, or the "inner world," then Introversion is your choice.

- **Intuition vs Sensing:**
The second pair of traits are based on how you gather information. The letter N is used for intuition as the letter I was already assigned to Introversion.
People who are intuitive are more interested in the overall context and are curious about patterns, concepts, and relations. If you prefer dealing with thoughts, looking into the future, generating new possibilities, or predicting what is not apparent, then iNtuition is

your choice. Sensors collect data from their immediate surroundings and rely on the things they see, smell, and hear. If you prefer answering with evidence, sharing what you think, having clarification, or explaining what you see, then Sensing is your choice.

• **Thought vs Feeling:**
The third pair of traits are your based on your decision-making style. How do you make decisions? Thinkers search for the logically correct option, while Feelers make decisions based on their desires, beliefs, and other people's needs. Unless you choose to use an empirical and unbiased approach to evaluate based on objective reasoning, then your choice is Thought. If you decide to use principles - i.e. based on what or who you think is important - then Feeling is your choice.

• **Judging vs Perceiving:**
The final pair of traits explains the lifestyle you're adopting. How is the world organised? Judges tend to be strictly governed in terms of structure and things, whereas Perceivers want items to be transparent and resilient and are reluctant to engage. If you prefer well-structured planning of your life, then

Judging is your preference. This should not be mistaken for 'Judgmental,' which is quite different. If you prefer to float, retain versatility, and respond to things as they occur, then Perception is your choice.

To identify your personality based on this method, your choice between the paired traits is either/or— you are either an Introvert or an Extravert; a Judger or a Perceiver etc. Once you have selected the style of each of the four dichotomies you prefer, you use these four preferences to create a four-letter code that sums up your personality type. For instance, someone with a choice for Introversion, Intuition, Feeling, and Judging would have the code "INFJ" (a preference for Intuition is indicated by an N to avoid confusion with Introversion). There are 16 possible combinations of styles of personality.

Most people find their letter combination by taking a personality test, but it is also possible to discover your personality type by merely studying your preferences and behaviours.

Myers and Briggs have been cautious in pointing out that no one combination is better than another; each personality has their unique talents, abilities, and contributions. It is also essential to understand that while some types tend to gravitate naturally towards specific behavioural patterns, the personality of an individual cannot predict their actions or what they are going to be good at. For example, while ENTJs are often assumed to have characteristics that we equate with leadership, if he or she has not acquired the related skills, an individual ENTJ may not be a particularly good leader. The type of personality can predispose a person to be a certain way, but the outcome is based on many other variables.

Additionally, unlike many other forms of psychological evaluations, there is no connection between the performance and any criteria. Rather than looking at your performance relative to other people's scores, the instrument's goal is to provide additional information about your unique personality.

## 2.3 Do your Rigorous SWOT Analysis

SWOT is an abbreviation for Strengths (Power), Weaknesses, Opportunities (Chances), and Threats, so a SWOT Analysis is a method to analyse a business according to these four aspects. You can use SWOT Analysis to make the most of what you have, to minimise chances of failure by knowing what you are missing, and therefore avoid the hazards you would otherwise be unaware of. Better yet, you can start developing a strategy that separates you from your rivals and thus helps you succeed in your market.

If you use your talents to your fullest extent, you will most likely succeed. Likewise, if you are aware of your weaknesses, and are able to handle them by making them insignificant in the work you do, you will encounter fewer problems.
So how do you recognise these strengths and weaknesses and evaluate their opportunities and threats? SWOT Analysis is a useful technique for you to do this.

What makes SWOT so important is that it can help you find possibilities that you wouldn't have seen otherwise with little thought. You can handle it by knowing your vulnerabilities that could otherwise hinder your ability to move forward and removing those risks.

Using the SWOT method, you will start distinguishing yourself from your colleagues and further cultivate the unique talents and skills you need to advance your career and help you achieve your personal goals. This tool gathers knowledge about your internal strengths and weaknesses as well as external opportunities and challenges. Treating your job as a company and yourself as a competitive product is essential to completing your SWOT analysis.

**Strengths**

To help you understand your strengths, imagine yourself as a competitive product in the marketplace. Personal skills are an advantage to you and can be used to differentiate yourself from others when you meet a potential employer or try to get your next promotion. Examples of strengths: excellent project management abilities, ability to improve or re-engineer procedures, exposure, and presentation preparation to large audiences, demonstrated selling capacity.

Answer these questions to help you identify your personal strengths.

- What benefits can you provide that others don't have (such as skills, certifications, education, or connections)?
- What are you better at than anyone else?
- What are your resources?
- What do other people (especially your boss) see as your strengths?
- Which accomplishments are you most proud of?
- Which qualities do you have that others don't show?
- Are you part of a network in which nobody else is involved? If so, what are your ties to influential people?

Understand the answers to these questions from both your viewpoint and the people around you. Get their point of view and suggestions. And don't be humble or timid – be as objective as possible. You can become happier and more satisfied at work by understanding and using your strengths. If you still find your attributes challenging to identify, write a list of your characteristics. Hopefully, some of these will be strengths!

**Weaknesses**
Weaknesses such as social vulnerability are a liability, and if they are recognised they can be addressed as an opportunity for growth. These are features that you might be able to improve to maximise future job prospects.

Answer these questions to help you identify your weaknesses.

- What activities do you avoid as you don't feel confident in doing them?
- What are your shortcomings according to the people around you?
- Do you have complete confidence in your training and skills? If not, where are you most vulnerable?
- What are your negative workplace patterns (for starters, you're always late,

you're disorganised, you're short-tempered, or you're stress-free)?
• Do you have personality characteristics that keep you in your field? For example, if you have to hold regular meetings; it would be a significant weakness to be afraid of public speaking.

Consider the answers to these questions from both an internal/personal perspective and an external perspective. Do other people see flaws that you're not seeing? Will co-workers in key areas consistently outperform you? Be rational – it is best to face your weaknesses as soon as possible, even if they are unpleasant truths.

**Opportunities**
Opportunities come in various types and shapes. Sometimes you've gone through doors without even knowing them. So, here are some things opportunities look for:

• Are there any significant changes/advances that you can take advantage of in your industry?
• Is there new technology or business development that you can use in the future?
• Is your organisation announcing a new job that suits your skill set? Or is a position that you desire vacant?

• Can you join a new initiative in your company that will help your career?

• Will you achieve a competitive advantage by acquiring new skills? For example, learning another language is an advantage in the airline industry.

Now is the time to reflect on external influences. Your list of resources may be personal or can be found within the industry.

• Look at the growth of the sector. Are there any influential people worth keeping an eye on? Maybe there's a new service that you or the company would benefit from.

• Are there business opportunities that are not being explored at the moment? Is there a more effective way to run a project, for example?

• Is there a fresh job opening at another company that you think you would be ideal?

• Are there any training courses that would make your job stronger?

• How can new technologies be of assistance to you? How can you use the internet to get help from others?

• Are you in a growing industry? If so, how can you benefit from the current market?

• Do you have a strategic communication network to assist you or provide useful advice?

• How do you see trends in your business? (management or otherwise), and how can you take advantage of them?

• Do you notice something important missing from any of your competitors? If so, can you use their mistakes to create something better?

• Is there still a need in your business or industry?

• Would you talk about something in your business with your clients or vendors? If so, may you offer a solution to create an opportunity?

You can find valuable opportunities in the following places:

• Networking activities, educational classes, or conferences

• A new role or mission that encourages you to learn new skills

• Expansion or acquisition of a product. Do you have specific skills that might help with the process (like a second language)?

Again, it's essential to look at your strengths and ask yourself if they open up opportunities – and look at your weaknesses and question yourself if by eliminating those weaknesses, you can open up even more opportunities.

**Threats**
There are certain things and events that bother you that could happen and discourage you either from achieving your goals or benefiting from them. You will need to recognise any potential barriers that come between you and your dream of success for this final part of the SWOT Analysis. You have to think about yourself as a company or commodity while doing a personal SWOT analysis and compare yourself to others. This way, the detection of threats is simple for you. Here are how threats can be detected:

•Were you held back by any of your peers?
•Is there someone on the team that makes the job more difficult? How could you deal constructively with this problem?
• Contrast with your colleagues. Were you overshadowed by a colleague who is more outspoken or ambitious? What will you do about it?
• Are there new methods or innovations that move the industry forward, but your lack of training keeps you behind? Think about how this can be repaired.
• What challenges are you facing at work at the moment?

- Do any of your colleagues fight you for assignments or positions?
- Does your work (or the demand of things you're doing) frequently change?
- Is the evolving technology a threat to your position?
- Is there any danger to your weaknesses?
- On a similar role, does one of your peers do a better job than you? Do you both compete for the same promotion?
- Is your career affected by the rise of new technologies or the decline of old techniques? Software engineering careers, for example, are usually stagnant because they have not spent the time studying the latest technologies.
- Do your characteristics hinder your career progress?
- What are the barriers to achieving your objectives?

The SWOT analysis will often include essential information - it can point out what needs to be done and bring things into context. A personal SWOT analysis is a perfect way to organise your personal development, prioritise it, and prepare it. It is not without its drawbacks, and it may need further in-depth analysis in its simplified format. But it is constructive and certainly worth your time as a quick and easy no-training tool that needs development.

A SWOT analysis, like any method of personal development, is not something you want to do every day. But if you find a particular problem that is very intractable, or you struggle to know where to start with a goal, it may be an excellent way to organise your thoughts and give you a different perspective on the issue.

## 2.4 Litmus Test your SWOT Findings to Find the Perfect Job

Once you've completed your SWOT analysis, you'll get a pretty good grasp of what is holding you back, things you should improve, what your ideal role looks like, and some of the factors that could hinder your career progress. That's where the real work starts — figuring what to do with that detail.

Knowledge of oneself can go a long way. If you are aware of the things you do well, you will do more of them. Understanding your limitations means you can find ways to close the gaps, whether it's taking a class or improving your processes.

You are using tools at your fingertips. "Working with leadership may help develop a plan that may include shadowing, mentoring, or direct guidance to help you improve," says Fowler.

"Fighting your threats from the same perspective means taking the time to investigate and staying one step ahead." If you identify a skill you know is in your chosen field, but you are weak in the area of power, you need to take steps to improve that skill.

- Specify the fields you excel in. Figure out what's right for you. Figure out what you see as your competitive advantage against everyone.
- Identify your shortcomings. Delve deeply to find the things or personal characteristics that you suck at, dislike, or even despise. Picture an office that you can't stand. In a worst-case scenario, write down the environment and the types of tasks you would be required to do.
- Specify how to turn your strengths into opportunities. Expand your powers, apply them to a list of activities you can perform daily, and watch how outstanding results can be generated.
- Describe how your shortcomings will affect your workplace fitness, attitude, and achievements. Do not hesitate to take it to another extreme – imagine your worst characteristics being

exposed at a meeting of the public or investors.

Keep in mind that how you view yourself and how those around you see you can overlap. But you'll likely be shocked by some of the findings. Depending on who you ask, the results will generally be different. Your family will focus on areas that, over the years, represent your home activity or historical achievements. You may also be more respectful or helpful – or maybe they will nag you for "being dirty when you wash the dishes," or otherwise. This is still a valuable lesson that could influence your life's other fields. You may be seen differently by your colleagues. The same applies to your managers (or subordinates if you have any).

Look for patterns after reading all of your gathered information thoroughly. Note how some of the answers are identical while other answers are entirely different. The detailed responses are either an indicator of the areas where you have evolved well or will help you become aware of patterns you didn't know about.

Specify your responses. Write down those that deserve further study or research. At the end of the day you will learn a lot about how people around you view you as a human being, a family member, a relative, or a colleague. This is a more realistic portrayal of yourself. You will get some reassurance or a new direction on challenges you should fix at work, and shortcomings you can eliminate, rectify, or convert into strengths after taking the quiz.

If you're serious about getting started as soon as possible, create a planner and put it into action. Identify where you want to be and look at the strengths and relationships that you can use to get there, and the limitations that you need to recognise - or resolve that might hold you back.

Prioritise and plan to neutralise your significant threats. If you've never done this, do it! Creating actionable strategies is a proven method that will lead you to success.

# Chapter 3: Learn the Art of Selling

## 3.1 Identify your Niche

Have you ever thought of making one of your hobbies into a business? Most companies offer a wide range of products or services but struggle to become the market leader for all of their products. Your proposal could concentrate on a small portion of potential customers rather than targeting a large population. Narrowing your scope gives you the chance to be the best at what you do.

You might combine your passion for knitting with your love of cats, for example, and start your own cat sweater company. Most often, pet owners are your clients, and they might have a particular interest or need in…cat sweaters.

The customers you are targeting in this situation are representatives of a niche market.
If you are struggling to find your niche, use the following steps:

**Identify your passions and interests.**
At this point in the book, you should have already done this. Nevertheless, if you haven't,

make a list of 10 areas of interest and things that make you feel passion instantly.

Business can be challenging, and it will test you at some point. If you are working in an environment you don't care about, your chances of leaving will increase dramatically — especially as a first-time business owner.

That doesn't mean you have to find a perfect match. You'll stick with it if you're enthusiastic about some aspect of running the company. You might be not able to find the drive inside to persevere if you don't care about the subject.

Here are some ideas to help you determine what your passions and interests are:

> • How do you enjoy spending your free time? What do you looking forward to doing if you don't have free time?
> • Which publications are you subscribed to? Which areas do you want to learn more about?
> • What groups or associations are you a
member of?

Be frank with yourself, as the responses will cascade down to the next set of questions. Recognise the differences between those things in which you are good with and those in which you are just okay. Is it possible to develop an aptitude in the latter or a pipe dream? In this stage, put aside all judgment so that you focus only on abilities, not whether they will take you somewhere.

Don't just choose a niche because you're "interested" in it; to be sustainable, it should be something you've been passionate about for several years. Is this something you like doing in your free time, or would even do if you weren't getting paid for it? If this is the case, you're going to choose a profitable niche easily.

So, if you haven't already, get your notepad and a pen (or open a Word document) and start recording all your hobbies and interests in one list. Once it is written and your niche is chosen, start brainstorming on what you can do to make this profitable. To create a profitable business, you must identify some of the problems that your target customers are facing, then decide if you can solve them.

Here are some things you can do to identify problems in specific niches:

> • Have one-on-one meetings with your target market or idea-extraction sessions. Make sure that you identify or create a

framework to ask questions that will help you discover points of frustration.

• Peruse through LinkedIn, Twitter, blogs, or other niche-related sites. Then,

look at the discussions taking place. What questions are people asking? What are the concerns they have?

• Identify keywords for analysis. Explore various keyword combinations on the keyword planner of Google Trends and Google AdWords.

**•Investigate your rivalry**

The existence of competition is not necessarily a bad thing. It may show you that a lucrative niche has been identified. But, a detailed review of competing sites is required. Create a new table and record all the competing sites you can find.

Figure out if there is still a chance to stand out in the crowd. How would you rate your keywords? Is there a way to change what you have and create a unique offer? There are several indicators that you can enter in order to excel in a niche, even if other sites already cover it.

**• Identify low-quality content**

It is easy to override the competition in a market where other business owners do not create high-quality, informative content that fits the audience.

• **Opacity**

Through establishing an authentic and accessible presence in a market where other sites are faceless and unnecessarily bureaucratic, many web marketers have disrupted entire industries.

• **Lack of competitive pay**

If you have found a keyword with relatively high search volume, but little competition and paid advertising, there is an opportunity for you to disrupt the market.

•**Determine your niche's viability**

At this point you should have a pretty good idea of what niche you'll get into. You may not have narrowed your list down to a single topic area, but you've probably found some ideas which you're feeling pretty good about. Having an idea of how much money you can make in your niche at this stage is important.

So, browse through your niche's top brands. It's not a good sign if you can't find any deals. It could mean that no one was able to monetise the niche. If a good number of products appear in your quest— but not an overabundance of products— you're in luck. Take note of price points so you can competitively market your items.

Do note that you don't have to launch your company with your product offering. In your niche, you will partner with creators of products, marketers, and website owners to start revenue generation while working on your unique solution.

**Test your Concept**
You now have all the details necessary to find a niche, and the only thing left is to test your concept. Setting up a landing page for pre-sales of a product you are producing is a straightforward way to do this. You can then use paid advertising to drive traffic to this link.

If you don't get pre-sales, that doesn't necessarily mean you are not in a thriving market. It might be that your message is not entirely effective, or you have not yet found the right bid. Through using A / B split testing, you can maximise sales and find out if there is anything that prevents further activity of your target market.

Once you have established the viability of a niche, start developing a full-fledged website. You'll want to know how to build a blog and attract more traffic to your site to raise your revenue and increase it.

## 3.2 Prepare Yourself

What comes to your mind when you think of your future career? If you're like other individuals, you might picture a steady stream of jobs in one industry, each taking you to the next level of success.

Your dream job has an opening, applications are being made, and you couldn't think of a better position for yourself – it's like this job has been created for you! When we find the perfect role and realize how much we want it, it's incredibly exciting!

For graduates and young adults who go to work at their first real job, the prospect of coming into the real world can be very overwhelming — emerging into adulthood calls for a work-to-play balance. Balancing your professional and personal lives is essential.

Networking and taking advantage of every opportunity that comes your way is one of the main components to being successful. Establish a portfolio, gain real knowledge, learn how things are done correctly, and then execute every job you do with your best effort. If you are passionate about these steps and believe in yourself, you will ultimately get a job you love because you are trained and know the ropes. Get ahead of the game!

Next, you need to choose the career path you want to follow to properly prepare yourself for a successful career and future. You need to understand the reality that if you choose a particular career path, success does not only come from the financial benefits. You need to be good at what you are doing and enjoy it to be fully productive. If you do your job right and there's no one better than you at what you're doing, the money will inevitably come. So, you need to focus on what you're passionate about when choosing your career path. Choose one that will make you happy, don't just rely on the pay check you think you're going to get.

Here are five steps to plan for your future career:

### 1. Know your opportunities
In the past, it was adequate to stick it out for 30 + years in one organization before you retired. No longer so. Ditch the static approach and embrace a more open mentality, because future employers prefer curiosity, genuine interest, and the ability to understand the viewpoints of others. It will help you better manage the ever-changing business climate by being able to go with the flow.

## 2. Embrace the defects

Ideally, your job will look like a series of carefully crafted work experiences, each which provides a better (and better paying) position as a steppingstone. Yet real life doesn't work that way, and there will be times you make mistakes by taking a job or trying out a career you thought you'd love, but don't. Rather than beating yourself up about it, learn to embrace your mistakes and learn that in retrospect, failures are never really mistakes.

## 3. Ignore the negatives

If you declare that you are looking for a new job (or even trying to find a new career), there will be those who will cheer you on and will be delighted if you succeed. Sadly, these people can seem few and far between. You may find that most people are "Negative Nancys" and are going to try to squash your dreams. But if you've been dreaming all your life of being a teacher, you should pursue your passion. The reality is that when someone else wants to pursue their goals, people often feel threatened, so don't mind them as you follow your dreams!

## 4. Take time

Your entire career is based on years of experience in different jobs and positions that you've held. So, for finding the perfect job, there's no reason to rush into it. If you want to be proud of a career, it's essential to take your time and find out what you'd like to do, especially if you've lived up to this point with ho-hum employment. Ask yourself what you would like to do if money wasn't an obstacle, then look for ways to find work in that area. Or even turn different aspects of your interest into a lucrative job — and a fulfilling career.

## 5. Prepare yourself

It can sometimes seem like a feast or famine in today's job market — and that's because it often is. That's why you need to make sure you're both financially and emotionally able to ride out the hard times. And even if you're working, you should always be ready if you lose your job or don't get the boost you've been waiting for (and counting on). So, put some money off to the side to get you through your job search and be ready to negotiate pay when you get a job offer. Be thankful for your future (financial) self.

## Tips for College Students

Being pragmatic in your job search is always a good idea, and this is especially true when planning your career. For college students or recent graduates, you're investing in yourself and your career for years to come by making smart moves now!

One common misconception is that after college, the professional experience starts. This incorrect career advice for students can and will cost them jobs for the future. Once you graduate, start looking for opportunities. Don't resort to the traditional "college student" or minimum wage jobs automatically. Search for a job that correlates with what you majored in. For example, students of journalism may benefit from working in a print production facility. It offers an inside peek at how the company works. Students in accounting may want to work at the local tax office as a receptionist. Majors of art history could volunteer at a local gallery or do an internship.

Students in college are studying multiple skills. Some of them have to do with their future career, while others might seem less useful. Open your mind to the so-called "useless" power. One day, those skills could come in handy. The goal is to extend your knowledge and abilities. Companies are looking for team members who can work in a variety of settings. To increase their marketability, anthropology majors may take a few business courses. Students in photography may want to take some graphic design or art classes to help improve creativity and their "vision" for art. Talk to your academic advisor to help you choose elective courses that complement your major.

While some occupations at the entrance level are more demanding than others, all jobs require work and training. Keeping up to date with technical and marketing advances gives you an edge over other applicants. Many graduates are more up to date with technology than seasoned professionals, giving them the upper hand. Nonetheless, the same students show a lack of awareness of industry trends. Visit your college library every month and read professional newspapers. They provide a thorough look at the changing landscape within your profession and will help you be better prepared for what is to come. Google provides a subscription to the news that can be tailored to any term or phrase quest. Establish an automatic search and receive monthly updated news updates in your inbox.

To become successful, most of this student career advice requires a few years of planning. Don't worry, there is still time to prepare students for the job search. The first move is to refine your CV. While it's best to plan for your future and have the ammo ready for your resume, it's easy to rewrite most skills and experience. Search for qualities that can be transferred (i.e., leadership, communication, team building, etc.) highlight such characteristics and related achievements. Using active action verbs show what you can do for the business. Treat your expertise as a selling product. Make the boss want you.

Preparing yourself is extremely important to achieve success. It would be best if you tried to enjoy the entire self-development process with all its successes and failures, interactions, and the people you meet on the way to the top. Have fun and make amazing memories!

## 3.3 Market Yourself

Who are you in the world? What message do you want to send? The idea of selling yourself may not seem like anything you should be worried about, but it is a skill that must be mastered by everyone. Understand the fundamentals and you will be able to put yourself out there as an expert.

Your career's success is your own. You need to market yourself whether you are a solo entrepreneur, a company, or an employee. And to get going, you don't need to spend money. Focus on getting your name out there and creating a reputation to reach the next level.

You need to understand what you are offering to be competitive in the job market to be able to market yourself effectively. It's essential to understand what makes you unique and how employers can express that. One way to think about this is: what would your personality mean about you if your name were a brand?

Marketing is often viewed as an activity related to companies, but it is at the core of every successful job search. You are developing your brand while at university. If employability is seen in its crudest form, we are all goods that try to sell our job market skills.

Here is the harsh reality: many applicants will apply for any position listed. Some of these candidates are going to be less qualified than you are, but some are going to be just as or even more qualified. In the face of this amount of competition, selling yourself is essential. This means you need to clarify why you are the best available candidate. It may feel uncomfortable to sell yourself, but it is indispensable. If you, as a nominee, do not show your best qualities, who will?

Talk like a marketer to conquer any feelings of shyness, pride, or discomfort. Create a marketing and sales plan for your job search as if it were one of the many drugstore aisle toothpaste choices. This will assist you in assessing your strengths, improving your success throughout the application process, and developing a strong identity that will make you stand out from the sea of applicants.

**Plan to have your skills remembered**
Display what you learn by building a base of information. Create your reputation and foster educated views. An expertise's hallmark is to find out what is essential and what are the facts. Develop relationships in your profession and culture with leaders and media members.

**Share the insights you have**
Contribute articles and blog posts whenever you have a chance. Assure readers that it is concise, well written, timely, and useful.

**Build a culture**
Build a network in your field of like-minded people and work on communicating and getting to know each other. Many experts are attracted to genuine experience, and you can open up a whole world of new possibilities in their businesses.

**Be at the disposal of others**

Become a trusted advisor and do your best to help as many people as possible. How can you use what you're doing to serve others? You might be able to offer your skills to a non-profit local company, or set up an internship or mentoring opportunity to help someone get started.

**Be socially competent**

Spend time focusing on social networking platforms in your industry, such as Twitter, LinkedIn, YouTube, Instagram, and other online communities.

**Share some of your experiences free of charge**

You can start building a fan base that trusts you and seeks expert advice from you.

Note who you are; this is the world's message. Each word you say, everything you express and do, is a message to the world. Just as a functional organisation protects its name, you need to protect your image by being careful about your words and actions.

**Identify your strengths**

Think of this as a product definition— in this case, it's you! When are you shining in the office? Consider the tasks you are performing well and try to remember on-the-job compliments. Look at your curriculum vitae and list your talents, abilities, and achievements. Think about why you've been pursuing your profession as well: why do you care about it? Try to talk and communicate about the things that make you excited and the work-related tasks you most enjoy about your job. Spending time on identifying strengths is worthwhile. Later on, your observations will help you write your cover letter and answer questions such as "Why do you want this job?

## Dress the part

Your talents are more important than your appearance, but the way you dress and carry yourself is a fact that plays a role in the success of your job search. To think like a marketer again, packaging design matters — often the most significant difference between two shampoo bottles is price or packaging, not the actual shampoo formulation. Make sure you wear appropriate attire.

## Create an elevator pitch

The elevator pitch is a short, often less than a minute speech about your background and experiences, and what kind of work you are looking for. During networking events, social opportunities, and job fairs, you can use your elevator pitch.

**Determine your unique values**

Spend some time contemplating what makes you different from your peers— your talents, interests, and ambitions. If you quit your job today, what would your company and colleagues be missing? Remember who you are and who you are not.

**Find out how others see you**

Ask trusted peers, colleagues, and friends to characterise you using four or five adjectives. What are your best qualities? Do they see you as irreplaceable, and if so, in which areas?"

## 3.4 Create a Portfolio

What if people in your network started saying, "I see you everywhere." And you get unsolicited calls from potential customers, invitations for guest appearances, and partnerships with other influencers you wouldn't have known about otherwise? Via media coverage, this can happen.

There isn't much of a barrier to becoming a media outlet these days. If you opt to do so, you can create videos from your smartphone, a podcast from your home computer, and write blogs directly from your laptop. It's a chance for you to relay your experiences through a medium that best shows your talents - whether through video, audio or in written word.

Let's talk about social media, which makes finding new audiences more straightforward than ever. You can post your information on social media platforms if you choose to make that your sole content. But make wise use of your time on social media. Instead of being everywhere all at once, select one forum and do a great job of communicating with new people, sharing your message, and adding value.

Some people carry out background checks on others when they want to buy something, bring interview them, or do just about anything with them. To do our research, we Google people.

**Activate a LinkedIn profile**
To market yourself, LinkedIn is one of the most energetic online resources because it helps you promote yourself. Too many LinkedIn members have what we'd call 'buttoned-up' profiles. Their profiles look like a rundown or a bio and they're written in the third person. You need to distinguish yourself with greater versatility if you want your profile to stand out. There is a much better chance for you to make a human connection with your audiences when you customize your LinkedIn profile.

Completing and customising your LinkedIn profile can go a long way in improving your marketing power, but enabling your profile will eventually enhance your reach and influence. Billions of views of LinkedIn profiles are growing and growing each year. Profile views of the right people on LinkedIn lead to good things like new interactions, discussions, inquiries, and incentives. You won't need to advertise yourself publicly when you use a LinkedIn profile.

## Publish Your Thoughts and Leadership Insights

Thought leaders are leaders who openly share their thoughts and build on their ideas. Through publishing thought leadership content, social media is now one of the most potent ways to influence others - both personally and professionally, and one of the most powerful ways to promote yourself and develop your influence. A person's or business's ability to share knowledge quickly across a broad audience has made the various social networks incredibly dynamic tools.

The most successful marketing happens when people don't realise you are selling something to them. After all, all kinds of marketing messages are seen throughout the day by the average American. Your goal is to communicate frequently, but not to be overbearing about it so that your message subtly sinks into the minds of people. If you do this, they will think you're great!

If you want to be known as an influential person in your industry or niche, it doesn't matter if you're going to sell more products, get more leads, drive traffic to your website, find a good job, get more clients, create your brand, sell tickets to an event, receive funding, venture capital, or sponsorship dollars.

Whether you're starting a new undertaking, a company, or working on expanding your existing business, social media branding should be essential to your strategy. Just about everybody you could expect to grab as a client already uses social media, so why don't you use it, too? A stellar presence in social media takes much more than just setting up a few accounts and waiting to find new customers.

Do not miss this excellent opportunity to engage your audience and make them lifelong fans of the company. Alternatively, use the branding tactics of magnetic social media to cut through the noise, push more leads, and outshine your rivals.

Don't think that the amount of stuff you write is the only thing that matters. To hold your following, you have to post regularly. But two or three times a week, perhaps even two or three times a month should cover you.

Social media is about telling the stories of your friends, and if you add some of your personality into it, people will respond better. Make your post amusing if you're funny. If there is a crazy story behind it, tell it. Friends come to your profile for you, so it's essential to bring a little more of YOU into the work that you do.

Also, to be seen and heard in the sea of things people see on their newsfeeds, you have to work as much as you can, so you have something a little different to offer. If you can add a picture, sound clip, or video to anything you do, do it. If you're not proud of what you're doing, then nobody else will care.

When you think a blog post you've written is the best thing you've done in a while, say it. "Check this out, I've been working very hard on it," demands a lot more respect. After all, there won't be any music if you don't toot your own horn every once in a while. People need to feel like they are getting something out of engaging with your posts.

If your content contains a lot of commenting on it, be sure to respond. Not only are you communicating to your audience that their opinion matters, but you are also engaging in debates, and getting constructive criticism that can enhance what you do. If any of your mates are doing similar things, be sure to check them out, comment, and share their work as well. You never know when they might return the favour.

Surprisingly, a lot of people forget to do this. Using your social media channels to pimp out everything you've ever worked on is tempting, but you have to use it to live your life also.

Use the customisable posting features on each social media platform to share content. It includes the title, image, and explanation of the content you post. Each marketer and user of social media competes to catch the eye of the consumer. The more structured your post is, the more successful your social media marketing will be for a particular platform.

For example, you have the opportunity to create a post that sticks out if you share a link to Facebook. All you need is a good headline, a clean, appropriate picture of value (which may be different from the image featured), and a short, persuasive summary.
Branding success in social media means getting more people to know the brand and enjoy it.

One of the best ways to make this possible is to create shareable content. People will keep coming back if they know that when they drop by your page, they will always find something they want to share.

There are many ways in which excellent content works for you. It steers traffic away from potential leads, while establishing your authority between customers and other professionals in a given niche.

The dedication it brings gives you and your audience deep insights into your niche. Nowadays, for very little money, small businesses can kill it — thanks to social media.
We all know that tweets are more engaging with pictures. We have known for a while that Facebook pictures are more engaging. Also, photos are becoming more active on LinkedIn. Three of the social networks that are "new "— Pinterest, Instagram, and Snapchat — are entirely based on photos. So why don't you use visuals to promote your content? Don't just build a "featured image" branded for sharing with your message. Create different photos in your content for each of the main points. Use these while posting on social media frequently.

## 3.5 Get your Dream Job

Understanding what you want is the first and most crucial aspect to getting anything you want. You're never going to find your dream job if you don't even know what it is.

You need to sort through the noise and concentrate on realistic goals to get the work of your dreams. Once all the steps listed above have been completed and followed, congratulations are in order as you are on the way to getting your dream job.

Usually, you have your resume and a few go-to cover letter templates ready to go when you're looking for jobs. But then comes a time when you're not looking, and then your dream job appears — a friend sends you a job listing that she feels would be ideal for you, or you see a tweet that says "We're Hiring" from your favourite brand.

Look at this brief guide to help you get closer to the upcoming job vacancy:

> • **Study the business in depth before doing anything else.** Make sure that you are well prepared for the entire application process by finding out as much as possible about the business you are applying for. This does not only mean searching through the website. Go deeper by engaging with the social media profiles of the company and get an understanding of the team culture.

Browse through some feedback on Glassdoor and read up on their rivals and different points of the business. Glassdoor is both an online job board and a website of workplace analysis. Because of the prominent role that employee reviews play, it is distinct from other job boards. Job seekers visiting Glassdoor will see written feedback, ratings, and client salary information before applying.

• **Brush up on the summary**. The next move is more precise: it's time to clean up your review, and make sure your LinkedIn profile is ready to make an impact while you're at it. First, do the easy stuff. Make sure that you use the best verbs to explain your experience and measure each of your achievements. Using what you know about the organisation, customise your resume as much as possible as you're editing (yes, it's okay to have slightly different versions of your resume for every job you're applying for). Eventually, complete your edits by making sure that the formatting of your resume is succinct and easy to read.

•**Reach out to people in your network now**. It's time to recruit your secret job-hunting weapon: your network with your revised curriculum and some company information. If someone you meet (or someone they know) works for the organisation or knows someone that does, it's time to reach out to them. Your main objective should be to learn about the business or your potential role as much as possible - but it's even better if you can get an "in" with the hiring manager! Find some people you meet and ask if you can get suggestions, thoughts or have a half-hour of their time for a quick chat. With any luck, you may be able to send your resume internally rather than apply directly. That said, if it seems like it might take some time, don't wait for this to happen.

• **Craft the ultimate cover letter**. You will need an expertly crafted cover letter, whether you are referred internally or are applying directly. Figure out who you should send the message to get started, then carve out 45 minutes to concentrate and start writing. Check out the Pain-Free Cover Letter Builder from The Muse (Google it). Reread it once you've completed it and make sure you don't make any of the seven cover letter mistakes that make recruiting managers cringe.

The fact is, far too many workers narrowly interpret their work. Once they have overcome it, they believe that they are good to go as long as they work hard. This couldn't be any further from the truth, of course. We live in a world of stagnant wages. Businesses outsource all they can. You've built up an expert reputation, and word is beginning to spread around your company. Now it's time for the right people to take the final step and be heard.

# Chapter 4: Pushing your limits

*"Push yourself to the edge of your limits. That's how they expand"* – **Robin S.Sharma.**

## 4.1 Adjust Mindset to your Goals

It is necessary to set goals to get ahead. Your goals are guiding you and they are giving you meaning. Sadly, goal-setting isn't achieved by everyone. What most people around you don't understand is that their negative attitudes and beliefs can hinder your mindset. If you have a pessimistic disposition, it's time to change your approach. Changing your perspective is easier said than done. Anything that entails a significant level of change is daunting and requires discipline and daily dedication.

One of the easiest ways to promote a positive attitude is to choose carefully who you are spending time with. It is essential to be in the company of optimistic and likeminded people. It will improve your strength, morale, and joy if you spend time with positive people. It also goes a long way to stick around people who share the same dreams as you do. Even when the going gets tough, it makes a massive difference because positive people can help you see the good in the fight.

A person with a stable mind believes that he or she is born with individual skills and has no influence over his or her creation. An individual with this mentality can avoid obstacles, avoid errors or failures at all costs, and give up quickly. On the other hand, an individual with a rising mentality accepts challenges, sees the effort as the key to their success, and believes that errors and failures are all part of the learning process.

It is essential to have a positive attitude to help change your negative attitude. Change your way of thinking and change your life and career. Instead of giving up before you try, say:

"I have enough skill and experience to run my own business!"

"To fulfil my goals would be a challenge, but I'm up for a good challenge! I am going to do that!"

You may not know this, but your positive story already exists – it's time to release it and see your life and business reach new heights in the process!

Now that you know the negative things you are telling yourself about what you can't do, what you're not good enough to do, and how everything you do is all wrong, you can change your mindset to be optimistic - leading to a happier life and business! As your dreams and ambitions are realized, continue to imagine your life, do the research, and take small steps every day to make your dreams come true and achieve your goals!

You know that you can do anything now – so follow your dreams! Achievement of our goals requires a positive mentality. Successful attitudes are those centred on success, positive opinions of the mind, motivational inclinations, and good habits. Acquiring an idea of achievement is a sure-fire way to dramatically increase your chances of achieving your goals.

It's imperative to focus your mind on the positive aspects of your goal. It can be uplifting to find inspiration through others who have accomplished similar goals; it can help reinforce the confidence that your aspirations can be fulfilled. Find people you can speak with about how they accomplished their goals and seek out positive people to surround yourself with. If you are just learning to develop a positive mindset, this is a crucial step.

## 4.2 Visualise Yourself at the Next Level

Visualising the end goal in mind is an essential feature of an attitude of success. Imagining our success creates a powerful excitement that should not be underestimated. When the brain gets excited about achieving goals, we become more committed, work harder to achieve them, and are more likely to do whatever it takes to make them happen.

There are two steps you can take to identify your priorities:

**Picture Your Dreams**
Close your eyes and ask yourself what you want in your life and business (no dream is insane – the limit is heaven!), write them down, and keep writing until your page is complete. You will be surprised to learn what you want to hear and see in your mind! Let it out!

**Create a Vision Board**
Put all your dreams and goals in a visual collage using a calendar, a digital app, Pinterest, or even a large display board! A vision board is a method that helps to explain, guide and maintain an emphasis on a specific goal in life. It shows images reflecting anything you want to be, do, or have in your life. Small strategies such as this go a long way towards sustaining the

attitude of achievement and should not be ignored. An essential part of changing your mindset is always having a vision of the ideal life you have in your head.

It's recommended that you put the vision board somewhere where you will see it all the time. It's going to boost your mood and make you feel fantastic. It will also create tension in your subconscious mind as you are not yet physically where you see yourself psychologically.

Another essential technique of visualisation is to construct an image or picture of yourself as if your goals have already been achieved. If one of your priorities is to own a new car, take your camera down to your local car dealer and take a picture of yourself sitting behind your dream car's wheel. If you have a goal to visit Paris, find the Eiffel Tower's print or poster and cut an image of yourself and put it in the photo. We advise you to find or create an image of every aspect of your dream life. Build a vision or visual representation for every goal you have — economy, job, leisure, new talents and abilities, things you want to buy, etc.

**Different Ways to Make a Vision Board**

- Go through a bunch of magazines and cut out any images that attract you and your ambitions and add them to the physical paper board.

• Browse the Internet - particularly Pinterest for pictures and quotes that you are interested in and that match with your hopes and aspirations. Copy and paste them to a digital board.

•Build your vision board so that it is innovative and works best for you! It is necessary and helpful to build a vision board to achieve your goals. Bring it where you can see it every day. A great tip is to use your vision board to make a screen saver for your phone or laptop.

Visualisation is the secret to achieving your everyday goals, as it will help them come to fruition.

## 4.3 Push yourself

Do you work best when you put pressure on yourself, or do you do better without it? Do you have the drive to get something started or finished? Not pushing yourself takes less effort and helps you remain relaxed. But that's not the way to become your best self. So how do you motivate yourself to help you conquer your challenge?

Here are suggestions that will help you meet your challenge:

### See the Challenge as "Real."
First of all, to face a problem, you must see it as real — not as fake, because no one other than yourself has decided that it is a challenge. It has to matter, and you have to keep yourself accountable. There has to be a penalty if you don't meet the challenge.

### Set Your Challenge in Stone
Secondly, see the obstacles you face as set in stone. Just because you give yourself a deadline, rather than someone else giving you a deadline, doesn't mean it doesn't matter, or that you don't have to reach it. Any challenge you give yourself is aligned with your goals, values, passion, and purpose.

### Set Firm Deadlines
When you place a deadline on the calendar, you will see it as a "drop-dead deadline." You've got to meet it, "or else." What if you don't? Understand how you're going to feel and how it affects others.

- What's going to happen if you don't force yourself to do it?

- How are you going to feel and think about yourself if you don't meet your deadline?
- How will the people you might have influenced feel if you do not fulfil the challenge?

Deadlines will drive you to the next level. Although your goals must be practical, which means achievable, they must also stretch you — push you to the next stage. Create goals that feel a bit hard to achieve.

## Get an Accountability Partner

If you keep struggling to move forward, ask someone else to hold you accountable. Accountability partners provide a tremendous boost because they are helping you to build momentum.

## Track your Progress

Take a weekly account of what you did to achieve your goal. For example, if you rate your progress on a weekly scale of one to ten, you can remain aware of your progress. You're going to know if you're moving too slowly or quickly enough. It would be best if you forced yourself to speed things up when you see your productivity or activity deteriorating or plateauing.

**Keep up your Energy**
In this world, most people don't get what they want because they don't have the means to help themselves. Throughout the day, they peter out, get distracted or confused, or feel tired — and then leave. Their weakness can motivate you to regularly increase your strength throughout the day. Eat healthy foods, get plenty of sleep, relax, take frequent breaks, move your body, workout, do things that energize you.

**Make it a Priority to Fulfil that Challenge**
If you let everything else come before your challenge, you will never meet your target. Try to get to grips with it every day. Don't let your goal get in the way of life. It would help if you pushed yourself. You are taking challenges that make you feel happy and help you make your dreams come true.

## 4.4 Find someone to push you

If you don't drive yourself and you need a push, it's time to hire help. It's time to contact a mentor or an instructor, even if you don't want to, because you know you need to put in just a little more work

Think about athletes in the Olympics. They are constantly pushing themselves, but even if they are the greatest in the world, they know that they need an edge. This is where their coaches come in.

Coaches are employed by executives, entertainers, entrepreneurs, and advertisers. Sometimes coaches are recruited by employers. What's the reason? Maybe they want their employees to be stronger, get the drive they need, be more productive, move towards their best selves - and a coach is who can guide them.

Have you ever noticed you're inclined to act a little naughty when you hang around certain people? It may not be significant, but you might have an extra drink when you're around these people, or you encourage yourself to overindulge and eat things you normally wouldn't eat, or you slack off a little. Have you ever found that your attitude towards your relationship changes a little, too, after hanging out with someone who doesn't respect their partner?

On the other hand, is there someone in your life who makes you sit up a little straighter? You might feel a bit around this person, but it's because you want to be on your best behaviour, and he or she is encouraging you to be your best. These are the kinds of people you need to be surrounded by - people who make you aware of your image, your voice, your organisation.

People who motivate you, work with you, and make you believe your relationship takes precedence.

Think of people in your life who fill your bucket regularly. They're giving you new information and pushing you forward. Your life will change when you surround yourself with friends like these. You become more optimistic, more motivated, and more focused on your goals. You need to spend time with these people!

The people who surround you are typically made up of your friends and family. Although we can't pick our families, we can choose our friends — friends that we want to be more like, and friends that can help reinforce our strength and positivity.

A potential friend is someone who can help shape and improve your decisions to improve your life. A good friend is one who gives inspiration and strength. They are respectful and care how other people are treated, they are honest, determined, and they make their friends' lives a priority. Do you have friends like these? If you're thinking of your mates now, you've probably got someone you're leaning on. Are the feelings reciprocal, or is it a one-sided partnership? Finding a balance in your friendships is crucial, and you need to be learning great qualities from each other.

Such optimistic people will find their way to you as you become more positive and more like the person you want to be and be around. Before you know it, you will be surrounded by friends who will lift you up and you will separate yourself from the ones who bring you down.

## 4.5 Work on your weakness

We all have to face the facts here in this imperfect world; we are good at some things, passable at others, and bad at some things that might be important. If you're an entrepreneur, wanting to be amazing at everything can be very frustrating. Worse, you might think you've got to be good at everything because you feel like you are the only one that can make your company a success. Do you honestly feel that you are not good at all, and there's nobody else good either?

Recognise your shortcomings and embrace them. If you're busy denying your weakness, you can't turn your weakness into power. So, your first step is to understand that you have vulnerabilities and assess how prepared you are to face them.

Overcompensating with outstanding planning is the best defence against a weakness. For example, let's say you have a terrible sense of direction, and you tend to get lost, even if it would be a simple matter of asking someone else to help you find your way. So, you use technology to save yourself with a built-in GPS in your smartphone, notes on your computer, and as a backup, a third device such as a tablet where you downloaded maps for offline use.

The slippery slope of self-bashing is easy to slide down after an unfortunate meeting or presentation. You are not in a position to make reasonable decisions about your results while your head is spinning with "I should have done this or that" scenarios. Therefore, your best bet is to physically and mentally move away from the situation to gain perspective. Taking a walk outside is a perfect way to physically get away from the workplace. At least 24 hours before revisiting the case, try to give yourself a break. In order to kick your drive into high gear, it's essential to come to the table with a rational, emotionally neutral mind.

### Check your Perfection at the Door
Say it now: "I'm sorry, and I am aware that I am making mistakes." As much as we would all love to be the perfect employee who bags every Employee Achievement award that has ever

existed, it's simply not realistic. In reality, it will only lead to frustration when you are reaching for an impossibly high standard.

**Look Beyond Yourself**
We sometimes turn inward when we are in a self-critical mode. So, it can help shift your focus outward and engage with others to resolve your shortcomings constructively.

**Leverage Workplace Jedi Mind Tricks**
It is time to take action on your criticism after disarming negative self-talk and bringing your shortcomings into perspective. Using prompts is a great way to keep up with progress, without relying on willpower (which comes in limited amounts) or beating yourself up. An eye for the future should distinguish any self-criticism. The real goal of creating success is to be constructive.

## 4.6 Embrace bigger challenges

Sometimes the critical distinction between winning and losing is how successful people view their challenges. Successful individuals believe the obstacles they face give them the strength to live their best lives. This doesn't mean that success is easy. Obstacles can be seen as opportunities for a luxurious experience to manifest and to reach higher heights. Anyone who has achieved success has been faced with obstacles, but they followed the necessary steps to deal with the difficulties before succeeding with perseverance, resilience, dedication, and patience.

The path to success is always in great need of stamina and determination. Speak to those climbing those high mountains and successfully reaching the top, taking risks, neutralising their fears, and turning the unknown into the known. I've always been a believer in the saying, "There's always a reward in everything we do, but it always includes some difficulty. If you don't want to risk, don't expect a reward." Challenges are there to challenge you. Are you going to move forward and face them, or are you going backwards and running away? Are you going to give up when you face challenges and give everything you got?

Your path to success is not going to be easy; there are going to be many roadblocks. To be on top of the obstacles, you need perseverance and bravery. You're not looking for chances to magically appear; you're going out to seek them. The latter will motivate you to be successful and stay on track.

If there is something in any domain of life that separates professionals from amateurs, it is the willingness to accept obstacles and challenges.

Professionals see them as a power that will enhance them, sharpen their skills, and make them more precious. If you know something, the world will test you, and if you face the test with an openness and ability to be tested, you will find yourself creating more of a positive mindset.

When you have a willingness to be tested, it opens up your mind so that you can be ready for anything. In sports they call it "successful preparation." This keeps your mind open and helps you develop creativity to solve problems. If rivalry is your thing, the rivals will be significantly intimidated. To contend with an opponent, stand in front of him and say, "I'm ready for anything you have!" Usually, that's not a challenge they like.

The Buddha taught us that the key to life is enjoying what you have; and not wanting what you don't have. To be happy is to be interested in the life you have right here, right now. By taking life as it comes to us, there is freedom— the good with the bad, the great with the terrible, love with the loss, and life with death. If we accept all of it, then we have a real opportunity to enjoy life, appreciate our memories, and mine the gems for our taking.

## 4.7 Inspire yourself to action

"Never confuse motion with action." — Benjamin Franklin

How are you motivated to continue to work towards your goals, particularly when you are faced with challenges? While some methods can inspire you more than others, experimenting with different ways to find your inspiration is good practice. You can rely on one of these tactics to get back on track when the chips are down.

*"Action is the centre of performance for all."* –Pablo Picasso.

Often the ability to act and fail can help you boost your level of confidence. It is essential to your success to be optimistic. We are not saying it's going to be quick, and we don't mean it's going to be hard. But we want to say is it's going to be worth it. The joy of fulfilling just one of our goals is enough to keep us taking baby steps on our list for everything else.

Here are some strategies that you can use to inspire yourself to take action:

**Split your goals into smaller, more realistic steps**
"I find it best to take one step at a time and cross each obstacle as they come to you." — Michael Stuhlbarg

Especially if you work towards a larger goal, break it up into a series of small steps that you believe you can achieve.

**Celebrate and praise yourself after each move for a job well done**
You're more likely to remain focused on the job with small steps because your celebrations will always come.

**Know your limits**
"The distinction between ignorance and intelligence is that creativity has its limits." — Albert Einstein
You know yourself best, and only you can define your limits. If you're going too slowly, you'll know deep down that more action needs to be taken. Nonetheless, you could face burnout if you try to do too much. Find out that magic point where you can achieve goals without a lot of stress and stay motivated to continue to take action.

"One way to increase our willpower and concentration is to control our stresses rather than let them manipulate us." — Daniel Goleman

Some things might annoy you more than others. Stay rid of these circumstances when you know you need to take action. For example, if you're a social person, you might need to move away from friends and family during the time you want to work. When it's time to work, prevent distractions by asking for help in such things as surfing the net, stop surfing the net, video games, and television. Ask for the support you need.

"Never let your ego get in the way when you are in desperate need to ask for help. At one point in our lives, we've all been helped." -Edmond Mbiaka

**Don't hesitate to get help from others**
There is only so much you can do on your own in one day. Indeed, sometimes you're going to have to do some stuff on your own, but if there's any way someone else can help, consider the possibility and ask them.

**Find an exercise that energizes you**
"Movement is a therapy that causes improvement in the physical, emotional, and mental states of a person." — Carol Welch

Sometimes you will find that going into depression is a cycle. You may have trouble getting your engines going in the morning, or maybe it's the afternoon that makes you feel sluggish. Find some exercise in these periods that will re-motivate and inspire you.

A good exercise routine is one thing that can improve you. It will increase your heart rate and give your brain fresh oxygen. This will refresh you, help you think better, and make you feel more like doing your job.

## Keep a tight schedule

"The only way to efficiently utilise time is to schedule it." - Sunday Adelaja, founder and senior pastor of the Embassy of the Blessed Kingdom of God for All Nations Church in Kiev, Ukraine.

A clear program and structured plan can help keep you focused and on track. In the early stages of planning your goals, be very precise when determining what you need to do and when you need to do them. This way, you won't have to spend time figuring out what you should do next when you complete a move.

## Develop a practise of gratitude

The moment we open our eyes in the morning, we usually know what we need to do that day. To stay motivated, think about some things that you are grateful for while you're still in bed. Once we wake up, we are often frustrated by what we need to do and repair, and that becomes our priority. So, instantly changing the emphasis, thinking about what is good, will put you in a better frame of mind to tackle the day.

# Chapter 5: Surround yourself with passionate people

*"If you surround yourself with positive people who build you up, the sky is the limit "*      *– Joel Brown.*

Surround yourself with mediocrity, and you are going to become mediocre!
Think about it for a second. Let it sink in because it's an opportunity for you to be brutally honest with yourself.

All of the people around you are excreting different energies. When you remain with positive people, positive energy will reach you and make you a more efficient and always on the positive side of life, optimistic person. However, if the company you surround yourself with is filled with pessimistic and depressed people, they will also make you sad and drive your positivity away from you, making you more drawn to life's negativities and farther away from your ambitions and passion. Your company is what makes you and inspires you.

## 5.1 Surround yourself with like-minded people

It takes a lot of thought and action to form a group of people in your life that you can rely on regardless of anything. You need to actively search for them. Understanding what kind of people make you feel most safe, motivated, and comfortable is the secret to connecting yourself with like-minded people. The ones you can count on in this community are the people who fill your life with happiness and drive you to be the best person you can be.

Your inner circle encourages you to feel safe and motivates you to talk about your dreams and aspirations freely. They inspire you to communicate your needs more profoundly and aspire for excellence.

How many of you have found yourself wasting an entire day trying to figure out how to use Instagram's newest version? Or building an entrepreneurial plan? Setting up a pop-up shop on the market? Imagine how much time you might have saved if someone else talked about it with you. Sure, entrepreneurship is all about trial and error, but the amount of time that can be saved is of a tremendous value. Regardless of what you know, you're going to learn something more, and it's so much more than you started with.

If you want to reignite your passion, surround yourself with people who are inspired all the time. Your attitude is going to improve, and you're going to leave the conversation feeling ready to take the next step. Listen to their stories; and hopefully, you can learn one or two things. Think about it. If you're surrounded by people who are motivated to excel, enthusiastic about what they're doing, and extremely energetic, then that's infectious in itself.

Passion and energy combined work together to bring about prosperity. It is fun to hang out with successful people. As children are always told-"practice makes perfect." The more optimistic you think, the more you envision and discuss options, the more you dream and believe in the possibilities, the more likely you are to accomplish them. And guess what? In my experience, people like to help others achieve their goals. In reality, by surrounding yourself with like-minded people and having a positive mindset, you are likely to be at your next level of success at a faster rate.

You will gain endless benefits if you have a network of people (co-workers, relatives, colleagues, mentors, etc.) with whom you feel a real bond and understanding.

- You feel safe doing things on your own.
- Without fear of judgment or confusion, you can talk openly about your feelings, dreams, and problems.
- You are able to inspire and motivate people.

Like-minded people will see how important your interests, passions, and side hustles are to you. They're going to check your progress and help you drive over the moments where you're feeling frustrated.

That's another thing: if your friends don't bring you joy, you're allowed to take them out of your life. Just because you've been friends for ten years, you don't have to stick with them forever. You've got to do what's best for you, above all. So, tell the people who are making fun of your dreams, who think your interests are crazy, and who are continuously insulting who you are as an individual and independent person – tell them you no longer have space for them in your present life. If they don't care about you, you don't have to care about them.

## 5.2 Learn from your past job experiences

Having a degree is not enough on its own. Employers seek more than just technical skills and a degree of discipline knowledge. They value skills like communication, teamwork, and problem solving in particular. There will be a real advantage for job applicants who can show that they have acquired these skills. Learning, growing, and constantly improving is part of your job. See the learning opportunities in everything you are asked to do – even the administrative grunt work, and you'll get the most out of all of your experiences.

It is all about maintaining a positive and optimistic outlook to get through a difficult change or coping with a challenging project. Bosses want workers who are dealing with challenges with passion and determination rather than moaning and breaking down whenever an obstacle trips them up. Very likely, you won't be able to choose your staff, schedule, or the duration of your commute, but you can always choose how to respond to any non-ideal workplace scenarios that may occur.

When asked, "What expertise has your work experience helped you gain?" It's hard to find an answer right away at times. Also, this question is often asked - "What did you learn from your previous job?" Given their pure nature, these particular interview questions are important - allowing potential employers to change how well you learn from past experiences – errors and other circumstances that occur in your life.

On your job and life path, there are some life lessons you can follow, and they are:

1. Know what you are for— and what you're against. This gives your clarity. Stand up for perseverance, hard work, and never take shortcuts.

2. Don't rest on your laurels. Instead, always look beyond your comfort zone for something.

3. Believe in the strength of failure. It's the easiest way of learning. Only remember to learn from your mistakes and to not repeat the same mistakes.

4. Trust your inner compass, even if it goes against your naysayers.

5. Take the chance of putting yourself in a new role. Some people have changed and started a new career at the age of 30, 40 or even at 50 years of age! They've been taken to where they are now.

6. Look back at past experiences— but only to see how far you have come. Unless you

continuously retrace your last step, you won't see your next step forward.

7. Don't think about doing the unexpected.

8. Stay humble— but let people know when you've done something great. Giving credit to others more than taking credit is incredible, but take credit for yourself when it's your time to own it.

9. Never stop learning; it gives you confidence. The stronger you are, the more relaxed you feel.

10. A winner will never quit; a quitter will never win.

## 5.3 Work as a team

"My way or the highway," is not necessarily the mentality that managers are looking for. Teamwork is the way to go in this day and age. But what skills in teamwork are essential for the workplace, and how can they be shown in your resume?

Well, you're going to find out. Teamwork skills are interrelated skills that enable you to work in an organised group effectively. Teamwork skills are essential to managers since teams in many organisations are a basic organisational unit. Teamwork happens when people work together to accomplish common goals and use their talents.

## Communication

The foundation of successful teamwork is the ability to transfer your point across and to genuinely consider what other people want to tell you. It doesn't matter whether you meet in person, communicate through email, instant messages, or on the phone— you must be successful in exchanging information regardless of the medium. Besides, the nonverbal communication elements are just as significant. Great teams nurture a culture of clarity and mutual trust. Everyone has to feel safe enough to be able to speak. Team players must be able to communicate professionally, both emotionally and intellectually, verbally, and using body language.

Those who are good in delivering communication:

- Clearly explain their thoughts
- Listen carefully to others and do not respond unless it is necessary
- Make attempts to communicate their feelings without sounding threatening
- Try to feel or understand how others think, based on what they say or their body language
- Ask questions whenever they want clarity or are unsure about something

What matters most is how knowledgeable you are when it comes to dealing with problems that arise. Note, not allowing any disagreements to escalate is crucial— that's why the best team players are great mediators as well.

At some point, conflict in the workplace is something that we all witness. You will make or break your career when you deal with disputes. Remember not to let anger or frustration get the most out of you. You're trying to come up with a solution that ultimately helps the squad.

**Building relationships and listening**
You can only build relationships if you listen to the voices of other people. It is just as important to be careful about their enthusiasm and their lack of it. Relationships and listening capacity go hand in hand; without one, the other can't exist. Such people are also good at developing a sense of harmony within the community. We help build relationships with others, creating a cohesive team.

Making decisions may seem pretty straightforward. And that's the case when everyone agrees on the course of action. But often, opinions vary, and you may need to make an unpopular decision. What sets great team members apart from the average is the willingness to see the larger picture, set aside their egos, and work for the common goal. It is also essential to be able to make decisions to move things forward. While it may be essential to take time to gather information to make sure the decision is right, there may be a period when any choice is better than none.

## Problem-solving

The very concept behind a team is to solve an issue together. That's why problem-solving skills are essential for every member of the team. The ability to look at a problem from multiple angles and to allocate time and effort based on the capabilities of each team member drives the performance and success of the entire team. Task-focused people often can solve problems, mainly when the problem is related to the task.

Managers are searching for new ideas to solve the problem, and implementers are going to turn them into effective practice. Shapers will see the' big picture' and the overall strategy, ensuring that there is no change of direction in the solution to the problem. Many problem-solving skills require a level of knowledge and experience, while others are focused on analytical ability. In all situations, we are concerned with the ability to evaluate a given situation and produce a positive outcome.

Being persuasive and having the ability to influence others is not a character trait that needs convincing. It is a skill that you can acquire. It applies mainly to team members in the sense of collaboration, who must inspire everyone to contribute to achieving the team goals and targets. Reliable teams are effective because they can accomplish more than each team member would if they worked on their own. Something people tend to forget, however, is that you depend on others as much as they rely on you when you work together as a team. Display your commitment by adhering to deadlines, completing your duties, and accepting any challenges along the way.

## Respectfulness

Being respectful doesn't mean you have to like someone or agree with everyone. Please show your appreciation, actively listen to them, and don't take them for granted. Don't know where to start? First, learn the names of your teammates. Practise tolerance, as tolerance goes hand in hand with respect and understanding. Be open-minded and willing to learn new concepts and ideas. People of different racial, religious, or minority backgrounds make this world such a fascinating place to live. Also, you don't have to see eye to eye with everyone. Immerse yourself in as much variety as you can, and then shape your views.

## Collaboration with others

And finally, it's important to remember that all teamwork conditions are simply about collaborating with others. If you have excellent interpersonal skills and are therefore open to receiving input and developing from it, you will become an attractive person to work within a team. It's really as plain and simple as that.

# Chapter 6: A Glance at the Future

"Without technology, humanity has no future, but we have to be careful that we don't become so mechanized that we lose our human feelings." – Dalai Lama

Further work is being done as robots, automation, and artificial intelligence have been launched. Jobs are massively disrupted, and experts say a more comprehensive range of training and skill-building programs will be created to meet new demands. There are two uncertainties: Will well-prepared employees be able to use AI tools to keep up with the race? And is market capitalism going to survive?

Workers are anxious about their prospects for future careers as automation software, robotics, and other types of new technology disrupt workplaces. Through providing opportunities for professional development and training, companies that introduce new technologies will alleviate concerns and improve morale.

While most employees understand that technology will affect their way of working in the future, few can imagine precisely how these changes will look. As a result, employees are excited about the ability to learn new technology, but they also worry that technology will remove their current roles or prospects for future employment.

## 6.1 How the working environment is evolving

The work environment and industry trends are changing rapidly. We are seeing a shift in power as job seekers take advantage of their market position - and with their voice, workers can make an impact. However, as the technology matures, the way we work is evolving, which results in a wider range of available jobs for people.

- Increasing data pools would mean new job search methods. Machine learning is changing the way job seekers find relevant jobs. There won't be a blast of random online jobs anymore, but rather a more tailored and personalised experience. The trends report both the upsides and the risks involved in this new method.

- Non-tech workers' demands will increase. Employers will look to hire robust sales and marketing teams to turn technology into revenue as the technology industry matures. This pattern is well underway even now.

• The ageing population is likely to result in a lack of talent. It is unlikely that the current challenges of recruiting top talent will improve soon. For the first time in U.S. history, there are likely to be more senior citizens than children under the age of 18 in America by 2035. This shows how an ageing population can impact the potential competitiveness and employment needs of companies.

• Employers and job seekers are bracing for a recession. How are employers and the process of hiring affected by a recession, and what are the symptoms of a coming downturn? They need to look into certain indicators, such as Federal Reserve behaviour, treasury bonds, and the housing market.

• Diversity and inclusion initiatives must go hand in hand. In the coming year, surveys illustrate the need to address structural corporate cultural issues that make workplaces unattractive to women and are underrepresented by minority groups. The study addresses critical improvements in initiatives for workplace diversity that will forever have an impact and nurture an environment in which employees feel a clear sense of purpose.

• Artificial Intelligence is our friend, not the enemy. There is a growing consensus among researchers that AI helps people do their work better. Many functions today include teaming up with automation or turning over routine tasks to AI systems. At the same time, workers can concentrate on aspects of their jobs that are more "real" and potentially more important. The study on Job Market Trends sheds light on how AI is widely used in today's workplaces, what companies are investing in AI and the possible looming shortage of AI-related jobs.

• We see more women in leadership and executive positions – in both business and in the boardrooms of top global organisations. As countless reports of research show, though there is an upward curve of women as leaders, there is still more room for growth. The study on Job Market Trends offers insight into women's main developments in 2018 and the current status of women in the workplace as a whole.

• Growing data privacy concerns: while customers have long been worried about data privacy, workers may be the next group concerned as employers collect more detailed data than ever before. The Economic Research team sheds light on the forms of data collection by companies, how they are trying to use the data, as well as the risks and benefits associated with this form of data collection.

• A lower-than-expected gig economy: About 1% of overall U.S. employment is attributed to the gig economy, known for short-term contracts and self-employment. The study on Job Market Trends assesses why the gig economy has fallen short of expectations and what kind of jobs the gig economy contains today.

• Amazon proves local talent: When Amazon continued to expand its operations by announcing a second headquarters in 2018, it all came down to its ability to quickly recruit and employ people. In a report on the position of the U.S. population, it is found that more than 70% of job applications are looking for locations in the same metro area as the residence of the applicant. The recent business news and the Job Market Trends study show how important it is to build a good company for both the local talent pool and the surrounding amenities.

## 6.2 Insight on emerging technologies

Chief Information Officers (CIOs) and business leaders will identify and efficiently exploit emerging technologies for their net-new values to keep up with the rapid progress and transformation that is happening across all industries and remain ahead of their competition. The field of emerging tech is fast-moving and ever-changing, so it's hard to get a handle on the state of the different markets, not to mention using them to drive business innovation.

Nonetheless, you should keep an eye on what's going on in general and try to get a big picture of our little project's success. Look out for some of the most significant tech developments that have already started to change the world, and the foreseeable future won't stop.

Artificial Intelligence (AI) already has a significant impact on how consumers communicate with businesses through smart websites and bots, and these tools are becoming commodified and incorporated into daily work.

"The biggest impact across all sectors— from retail to healthcare, hospitality to finance — is felt as AI enhances data security, speed and accuracy in decision making, and employee productivity and training," said Maddy Martin, Corporate Vice President and Head of Growth and Education at Smith.ai. "With more competent workers, better-qualified sales managers, more effective problem solving, and systems that feed real data back into future processes and product development, businesses using AI solutions can use resources much more effectively. Best of all, as innovation and competition grow in the AI sector, costs are reduced."

Although a full-fledged, human-level AI is still a long way away, for years, we have felt the effects of limited AI. We see the controversy taking place live in the fast-food industry, where demands for higher wages fuel restaurant automation — Carl's Jr. CEO is investing in AI, and Wendy's is exploring the installation of automated kiosks.

Robotics with applied AI is the most appealing and helpful to human resources. The robots are programmed to perform a repetitive task that increases productivity and is used effectively. Amongst some of the activities that are risky for humans to do are bomb defusing - a unique feature of robots, space exploration, and programming. By using collision sensors, cameras, and ultrasound sensors, advanced research in robotics is able to make them see, hear, and touch. The robot is used in space exploration and is adaptable to the physical conditions and climate.

Artificial Intelligence is applied in daily life and is effectively growing around us in areas of communication, time management, education, learning, health, safety, traffic control, buying, marketing, shopping, and planning. In research, artificial intelligence is used to build experiments, train personnel, analyse data, and reduce complexity.

Artificial intelligence is a technology that is much more relevant than you know. It needs to be applied by every company in its website design, application development, and marketing process. In other words, both companies need to collaborate with creators of AI. For artificial intelligence, for example, game developers and gaming consoles are extensive. Yes, many of them are creators of AIs. This is because artificial intelligence makes it fun to play video games. Whatever video game you play, the program will provide you with an answer, and it will be customised by your feedback without human intervention.

AI robots are working on protocols. They do the job in the most appropriate way for what they are programmed to do without any feelings or emotions. Therefore, nothing can stop them. They perform their tasks with an accuracy of 99.9 percent that humans may not be able to match. Whether it is data analysis or necessary computations, it will be done with accurate precision by robots.

That's why some businesses are using them to analyse data. Recognise that critical business decisions are based on statistics for data analysis, and if the figures are not correct, it can be disastrous. Using AI for your company reports and data analysis will result in accuracy and intelligent forecasting.

With speed, which is their main characteristic, robots, machines, and computers operate flawlessly. Speed is one of the reasons why artificial intelligence technology should be exploited further. Take, for example, Microsoft Excel. To summarise hundreds of figures, all you need to do is highlight the characters and press the auto-sum button and the answer will appear in a flash. That's precisely how pace works for the robots. So, think about artificial intelligence if you understand the speed of computations.

Because of the danger involved, certain activities cannot be done by humans. Nonetheless, due to the importance of their performance, these activities need to be carried out. Robots are now doing such functions. Many explorations, for example, are dangerous due to the gasses that may be emitted by the act. In order to perform these tasks, it is easier to build robots than to risk human lives.

Robots are being built to explore space these days. They can take snapshots and return them to earth. Many robots are even able to fly their space shuttle. They have been specifically designed for the job, all based on artificial intelligence.

## 5G

The rise in 5G networks enhances our ability to move, access, and analyse data through wireless platforms. When 5G rolls out more thoroughly in the years to come, it will accelerate the production of more complex applications to solve problems and increase industry-wide growth.

"The implementation and introduction of 5G would allow a few innovations to have an impact on business, including wireless speed and latency for complex solutions such as driverless vehicles," said Michael Haines, group chair and director of Microsoft's partner incentive strategy and program design. "However, once fully deployed globally, 5G will help emerging markets reach the same' business speed' as their developed counterparts. Technology providers designing 5G-based solutions for specific industry applications will have realistic, early-moving advantages."

Serverless computing allows companies to build an integrated and abstract No-Ops IT environment. Serverless computing was fresh on the list this year, along with robotics, replacing quantum computing and automation.

"Block-chain came crushing down from its hype period height, and that's probably for the best," said Julia Moiseeva, a member of the community leadership group and creator of CLaaaS (C-Level as a Service) Management Solutions Ltd., in the statement. "Now that the excitement and the furore of the masses have vanished, the dynamics of the research around block chain have taken a full U-turn, again, for the better."

The report found that IoT drives business changes by providing the data needed to improve marketing, increase sales, and reduce costs. "Everyone in the technology world, as well as many customers, is hearing the word Internet of Things," said Frank Raimondi, a member of the leadership group of the CompTIA Emerging Technology Community that works in Chargifi's strategic channel and business development.

"It's an understatement to say it's confusing and daunting," he said. "IoT can mean many things for many people, but if they start adding related IoT applications for their existing and new clients, it can mean incremental or new business for a channel partner. Most importantly, they don't have to start from scratch."

Having mentioned some of the emerging technologies, a point to consider is that skilled workforce will be needed for all such tech operations and it is just matter of time when we will see the high demand of AI/ Robotics engineers, 5G Technicians, and Block chain computing experts to name a few.

## 6.3 What is the Green Industry?

Green Industry means economies that aim for a more sustainable growth direction through green public investment and public policy policies that promote environmentally responsible private investment. Industry greening is a way of achieving sustainable economic growth and fostering sustainable communities. This requires policymaking, enhanced industrial production processes, and efficiency that is resource efficient.

For several years, renewable energy sources, such as wind, solar, and geothermal, have had an impact on commercial sectors, generating more sustainable practices across the board. Renewable energy and creative energy supply approaches are now also more prominent in business-to-consumer industries. Companies can offset their use and costs by implementing renewable methods such as solar panelling, even in residential scenarios. Businesses are also seeking more innovative ways of generating electricity— one company is even transforming food waste and wastewater into energy that can be used.

Green business trends towards energy efficiency have an impact on the residential marketplace, especially with home renovations and homeowners' choices for home remodelling. Building companies and home service providers offer eco-friendly solutions favoured by homeowners. Common examples of these common eco-friendly goods include new high Energy Star appliances, tankless water heaters, solar panelling and replacing windows or using window film. Most construction firms often implement green industry practices in their design and procurement processes, such as using recycled or recycled materials for a range of home renovation projects, rather than brand new products and fixtures.

With an emphasis on carbon recycling, green infrastructure, micro grids, the circular economy, and the B-to-B sharing economy, green business patterns are expected to continue to grow. Progressively, these elements of eco-friendly business practices are becoming more of an opportunity to reduce risks and increase revenue— opening the door to funding sustainable business growth for mainstream investors.

Innovative solutions are being developed by many companies to help build a green future. They take this route to gain customer support and reduce environmental harm.
Industries in all manufacturing and industrial sectors are also developing strategies aimed at reducing waste and pollution by improving production and use of products on the market by end-users and customers.

To do this, different steps are being taken:
• Instituting waste reduction activities. Waste recovery.
• Buying remanufactured products, such as parts and equipment.
• Choosing alternatives to green goods.

• Green Product and Service Policy adoption.

Whatever way you choose to adopt green technology in the future, in order to stay competitive, you need to be at the frontline of emerging technologies and energy efficiency. Your company or association must comply with the current standards and regulations on performance, as well as the criteria for implementation. It helps you to adapt quickly to future changes in green technology solutions. Thus, ensuring a long-term career.

## 6.4 STEM Jobs remain the most important

STEM stands for science, technology, engineering and math. STEM is critical as it permeates all parts of our lives. Science is all around us in the world. Technology is expanding continuously in all aspects of our lives. Engineering is the fundamental structures of roads and bridges, but it also tackles the problems of changing global weather and making our homes environmentally friendly. In every profession, mathematics are involved.

We are growing a passion for it by introducing students to STEM and giving them opportunities to explore STEM-related topics and eventually find a career in a STEM field. A STEM-based program requires real-life situations to help the learner understand how and why things work. Programs such as Engineering for Kids combine multiple classes and provide opportunities for children to see how ideas apply to life and potentially stimulate a desire for a potential STEM career. STEM exercises give the students practical and mind-on lessons.

Workers in science, technology, engineering, and mathematics play a vital role in the U.S. economy's sustainable growth and stability and are a critical component to help the U.S. win the future. STEM education develops critical thinkers, increases the literacy of science, and encourages the next generation of innovators.

Innovation is leading us to new products and processes that benefit our economy. STEM fields rely creativity, science literacy, and a strong knowledge base. Most future jobs will require a fundamental understanding of math and science. Given these persuasive statistics, U.S. students are lagging behind other developing countries in math and science.

Here's why STEM education for young students can be so critical.

STEM education helps bridge the gaps between ethnicity and gender that are sometimes present in math and science. Initiatives have been introduced to increase the role of women and minorities in STEM-related areas. Traditional gender roles are disrupted by STEM education. STEM education and employment must be a national priority to compete in a global economy. Each decision made uses a STEM element to understand the implications.

STEM education is vital in helping all global economies at the forefront of world leadership. Unless STEM education is not strengthened, the economies will continue to fall down due to the lack of math and science-related industries in the world, and so countries will struggle to maintain a global position. STEM school education is essential to stimulate interest in students pursuing a STEM career. Teachers, however, do not bear the entire burden of STEM education. Families must also encourage their children to undertake STEM programs, raising awareness and interest in the benefits of STEM education at home and in extracurricular activities.

STEM is critical because it is connected to our planet: the economy, our general well-being — all backed by science, technology, engineering, and mathematics.

Now, there is a disparity between high-demand employment and the skills needed to fill them - and this gap will only expand if nothing is done about it. In the next decade, 80% of professions will require a deep understanding of STEM skills. Furthermore, fewer and fewer students go beyond the STEM skills needed to succeed. Some of the students struggle to meet the necessary mathematical skill standards, and most students choose not to take elective or advanced courses required to continue in the STEM field. So, what is the product of this current trend in behaviour? There are plenty of jobs that require a comprehensive understanding of science, technology, engineering, or math (or all of the above) and there would be no one to complete them.

We have heard about the tech boom that is happening right now, and we can even see it going on right in front of our eyes. Every few hours, there's a new gadget out there, and it isn't easy to keep up with the trends. These trends, however, help boost the economy, create jobs, and keep money in our pockets. To help develop the next useful antibiotic or cure for a disease, we need professional STEM experts. To build the next new phone or a computer that learns faster than a person, we need engineers and developers. We also need those math-savvy people to help us understand big data, make sense of our economy, manage finances, and even help us get to Mars!

To remain competitive with their markets, businesses need to have top talent. Companies are so keen to hire those who will help them stay relevant now and in the future. This means they need the best Research and Development departments, the best accountants, the best engineers, the best web and app developers, the best designers-you see where we are going? The best of the best! Industries around the globe are now investing in STEM education programs in hopes of being able to develop the next generation of innovators.

Now that we've spoken about the longer-term importance of STEM education projects, talk to your children about the importance of these services - right here and right now.

Mastering STEM skills will also build the strengths and skills your children need to develop for any future career they might want to pursue. Students develop their research questions during STEM training and adopt a process that helps them learn to consider multiple perspectives and relate ideas to solve a problem. Whether it's the Engineering Design Method, the Design-Thinking Process, or the Scientific Method, your kids should collaborate with others; ask essential questions; take leadership in their roles and test several hypotheses to find a solution.

## 6.5 Technology's Impact on Labour and Employment

Machines these days are so efficient that they can easily take the place of humans to do a job, and the skills of a human can be replaced. And it's not just about boring, low-skill jobs. In recent times, automation, robots, algorithms and artificial intelligence (AI) have shown that they can do the same, or sometimes an even better job than humans who are dermatologists, insurance claims adjusters, attorneys, oil field seismic testers, sports journalists and financial reporters, crew members on guided-missile destroyers, hiring managers, psychological testers, retail, and on-board salespeople. Furthermore, there is an increase in fear that technological developments on the horizon will destroy jobs of the millions who drive cars and trucks, analyse medical tests and data, perform middle management tasks, dispense medication, exchange stocks, and assess markets, combat on battlefields, perform government functions, and even replace those programming software, that is, algorithm makers.

The latest research paper by Daron Acemoglu and Pascual Restrepo, Acemoglu, D., & Restrepo, P. (2017), found that "one more robot per thousand workers reduces the work-to-population ratio by about 0.18-0.34 percentage points and salaries by 0.25-0.5 percent." A central question about the future is how formal and informal learning systems can be established to meet the changing needs of people who want to attend future work-to-work requirements.

Recent advancements in machine learning and artificial intelligence that gave us Watson and self-driving cars mark the start of the world's seismic shift as we know it. Yet significant innovations have been around since the beginning of recorded history (defined as commonly used inventions that improve over time and have spill over effects that cause more progress). Such devices (known as general-purpose technologies, or GPTs) have changed the course of history, ranging from the first metal tools to the wheel and press. GPTs "interrupt and accelerate the normal economic growth march" Helpman, E. (2019). In other words, they make people more competitive and lift living standards. They also help to open new kinds of job avenues.

Today's average American has better medical care, greater access to information and education, and better ways of interacting and travelling in the not-too-distant past than the wealthiest people in the world. We also have undergone a dramatic increase in living standards, whose "economic efficiency is the most important single determinant across countries and over time." The Economic Advisers Council provides us an indication of remarkable changes in agricultural productivity over the past two centuries: "In 1830, a farmer's output of 100 bushels of wheat took 250-300 hours. It took just 40-50 hours to produce the same amount in 1890, using horse-drawn machines. By 1975, a farmer could produce 100 bushels of wheat in only 3-4 hours with giant tractors and combines." By generating more output, with the same input value, agricultural machinery reduced the cost of production. As a result, food became more affordable, making people less likely to die of hunger. However, the increased productivity from agricultural work automation led farmworkers to move to towns, where they helped develop and grow the industrial economy — the production of new goods and services and the rise in consumption. Productivity has increased even more as automation has reduced costs, making housing, health care, schooling, and government more accessible.

Technology has increased the size of the economic surplus cookie and has redistributed much of it to customers. Take one example: although Amazon offers free delivery on the same day or next day, delivery is not free -- there are significant resource costs for Amazon to accomplish this. The benefits from Amazon's technology investments and changes in its supply chain are expressed as a combination of lower prices, increased choice, and faster delivery, as the company is fighting to win over customers. From this viewpoint, we can understand how it is understandable that William Nordhaus reports that a whopping 96% of technological advances go to customers, not to manufacturers.

As impressive as the technological advances have been, they also occur against a backdrop of rising inequality, a shrinking middle class, and job-finding difficulties. From the 1940s to the 1970s, all-level incomes in the United States rose at about the same rate. Since then, however, the wealthiest Americans have seen significant gains in their revenue and wealth share, while much more modest gains have been seen in the majority of the income distribution. Consequently, as the middle class in America has shrunk, the country has been devastated by a horrific opioid epidemic in areas of high unemployment.

It is, therefore, essential to remember that automation has no uniform effect on employment; a computer can either be a replacement or a supplement to human labour.

A machine will replace human labour if it is capable of producing more for the same cost (such as its wages) than the worker, or as much for a fraction of the price as the worker. This is most likely to happen when the tasks of a worker are repetitive and codifiable— that is, when it is possible to translate the instructions for the functions into code for a machine to execute. However, in simpler, controlled environments, automation is more able to replace jobs. Although computers can perform the most complex calculations in milliseconds, having a machine write novels or care for children as effectively as humans do is much more difficult.

Machines supplement labour by encouraging workers to be more efficient, but they cannot replace the worker entirely. In other words, the technology that complements human labour makes it easier for people to do their jobs and focus on what makes people exceptional, such as generating ideas, problem-solving, pattern recognition, and complex communication— all of which are the shortcomings of computers. For example, calculators, spreadsheets, and software for bookkeeping all made the work of accountants much simpler. Nonetheless, for the most part, humans are still the ones who provide feedback and strategic advice to the businesses they are working on.

Our world will be changed by developments in Artificial Intelligence (AI) and Automation. The current debate focuses not on whether such changes will occur, but on how, when, and where the effects of artificial intelligence will be most dangerous.

We need to be concerned about the effects of artificial intelligence and automation. Although technology is not necessarily good or evil, it has an excellent capacity for both in the hands of humans.

In some situations, technology may make an employee's job obsolete so that it no longer makes sense to hire multiple employees. On the low side of the skill continuum, job demand (i.e., milkmen, switchboard operators, mail-sorters, dishwashers, ice-cutters, weavers, and assembly line workers) has dropped dramatically–or even vanished–due to innovations such as refrigerators, cell phones, and industrial machines. While the advent of these inventions has pushed jobs out, it has also allowed us to make certain types of work more bearable. For example, restaurants do not need as many human dishwashers by investing in industrial dishwashing machines. As a result, competition would be decreased for dishwashing workers, although some would remain. It would then eliminate these remaining jobs. The human dishwasher would only have to load and unload dishes instead of doing the actual washing by hand.

Although considering other low-skill jobs dying out due to automation — as robots now can vacuum rooms, patrol houses, and flip burgers (to name but a few tasks) — machines are still not replacing low-skilled cleaning, defence, and food service jobs. This is because while some tasks may be automated, computers cannot take over whole responsibilities. For example, while dishwashing machines do an excellent job of washing dishes, in the process, humans are not entirely replaced, because computers do not load or unload themselves. People are still outperforming machines, especially in jobs involving manual skills and different environments. Therefore, the demand for low-skill jobs is still (and will be) there. As we will see later, in fact, demand is increasing.

Middle-skill jobs are more likely to be codifiable (including blue-collar manufacturing and managerial roles, as well as clerical white-collar sales positions). These have vanished as a result, while low-skill jobs have not.

Assembly line workers also replaced most artisans and craftsmen. Middle-skill jobs are replaced by low-skill jobs in this cycle of "deskilling." In the meantime, specific situations die out, causing employees to move to occupations where they are overqualified. For example, most job losses in manufacturing have been due to automation (as politicians tend to suggest, rather than international trade). Workers who had previously been hired in the manufacturing sector had to turn to lower skills and lower pay in the service sector to get through. This increases the growth of jobs in low-skill work.

Artificial Intelligence is a promising field of study (probably the most promising). The area is still developing, yet, it has achieved quite a lot since its inception. However, there is more to be done.

Candidates interested in pursuing a position in AI require special math, technology, logic, and engineering preparation. Particularly noteworthy, written and oral communication skills are needed to interact in industrial environments and to use AI tools and services. To acquire these skills, those with interest in an

AI career should investigate the various career choices available within the field.

Necessary computer technology and math backgrounds form the backbone of most artificial intelligence programs. Positions at the entry-level require a at least a bachelor's degree, while supervisory, leadership or administrative positions often require masters or doctoral degrees. Typical training involves the study of:

- Different math levels, such as probability, statistics, algebra, calculus, logic, and algorithms
- Networking Bayesian or graphical simulation, including neural networks
- Physics, engineering, and robotics
- Computer science, programming languages, and coding
- Cognitive science theory

Candidates can find degree programs offering different AI majors or pursuing AI specialization from significant subjects such as computer science, health information technology, graphic design, or engineering.

Artificial intelligence careers can be pursued in a variety of settings, including private companies, public organizations, education, the arts, health care facilities, government agencies, and the military. Many positions may require security clearance before hiring, which may be expected to handle depending on the sensitivity of information personnel.

Examples of AI professionals' specific jobs include:

- Software analysts and developers
- Computer scientists and computer engineers
- Algorithm specialists
- Research scientists and engineering consultants
- Mechanical engineers and maintenance technicians
- Manufacturing and electrical engineers
- Surgical technicians are working with robotic tools
- Medical health professionals working with artificial limbs, prosthetics, hearing aids, and vision restoration devices
- Military and aviation electricians working with flight simulators, drones, and armaments
- Designers of graphic art, multimedia artists, creators of movies, clothing producers, and architects
- Post-secondary teachers in vocational and industrial colleges, training centres, and universities

Artificial intelligence aims to improve the quality of life from its inception in the 1950s to the present day through multiple settings. As a result, those with the ability to translate digital bits of information into meaningful human experiences will find a career to be enduring and fulfilling.

# Conclusion

*"Massive, deliberate action is the way to success."* — **Tony Robbins.**

In conclusion, the main key here is to draw out the positive psychological features and refrain from negative elements based on the Myer Briggs personality test you did earlier. Do some reflection over the test results and gradually you'll grasp characteristics better suited to you. Although every role or business has some part of it we dislike, by using the test we hope to laser focus only those roles where you are an advantage, whether it's natural ability or skill set, and completely avoid the ones, which concentrate on areas which we loathe, exhibit inability or disinterest.

If you want to succeed, you can do it with purposeful action. Think about and take valuable learning's what you have done in the past to achieve your goals. We live in a more social environment than ever before. Once you've identified what you love, get busy on Twitter, Facebook, and LinkedIn, connecting with people who share an interest in your areas. Read blogs, enter forums, and learn how to do what you want to do.

It can be hard work to look for a job, as it's not just about finding any old job. Finding the right place is essential, a situation that is an excellent fit for you now. Either as an incentive or steppingstone for your career, you'll be content with it during the long haul. If it's the wrong job, if the position doesn't work out, you'll end up having to start the job search again. Besides being frustrating, when you write your resume, you will need to make sure it is focused in order to prevent you being called a career hopper.

Before making sure you want to work for a company, evaluate their job offer carefully. Do you want this job? Will you be able to do it? Is it going to boost your career? Will it give you the flexibility you need or the balance between work and life? Is the pay what you were expecting? If not, is there a way to negotiate a higher wage? Are the benefits of the employee sufficient for your needs? How about the work schedule, the hours, and the commute? If there is anything that makes you think twice about the job or the compensation package, the time to take action is before you accept the offer.

The best way to find a job that doesn't turn out to be a lousy profession is to find work that meets three criteria: ambition, ability, and need. I believe we should all aim for the intersection of these three qualities to pursue a vocation.

Ideally:

1. **Your work should make you happy.** You ought to enjoy what you're doing for work. Only do things that "spark joy. "

2. **Your job should make you money.** It's not a good thing to seek your dream if no one pays you. You need to be paid for your contributions.

3. **Your work should tap into your talents.** Your career should involve something you're good at; it should allow you to put your skills to good use.

When you seek to fulfil your highest career aspirations, there will be critics who will question your ambitions or voice their doubts. You need to block the distracting noise and concentrate on your path to be successful. In your career, you're going to get a lot of people who think it's very fresh and exciting. You will always have people who think it's crazy, and you're wasting your time. It's going to be difficult to watch these people make a lot of money in their conventional professions while you scratch and claw for the first few years. You have to have the mental maturity to cope with this.

You're going to be better off thinking about your future and happiness rather than thinking about the success of other people in more conventional careers. Talk to your close friends and think positive thoughts. Connecting to your unique interests and goals and getting to know your authentic self gives you power that others don't have in your chosen profession.

It may not always be easy, but you can achieve whatever objective you set out to accomplish when you stay motivated! While you may think you're too young to worry about your future career, you need to start thinking about your post-secondary life right now so you can take the steps you need to get into whatever profession you choose.

When you finish high school, it may seem daunting to try to choose a business, but social media is full of success stories. Also, always keep in mind that changing your career path is never too late as we read countless stories of others that have achieved their dreams regardless of age. In closing, do not overthink your struggles, be observant but remember quality takes time, live an authentic life, and keep in mind this will help you to achieve your dream job.

# References

1. 7 Impacts of The Artificial Intelligence Technology. (2019). Retrieved from https://towardsdatascience.com/7-impacts-of-the-artificial-intelligence-technology-5a4663397961

2. Research, F. (2019). Breaking down the 10 need-to-know emerging technologies | ZDNet. Retrieved from https://www.zdnet.com/article/breaking-down-the-10-need-to-know-emerging-technologies/

3. 7 Emerging Technologies You Need to Know More About. (2019). Retrieved from https://www.herox.com/blog/718-7-emerging-technologies-you-need-to-know-more-about

4. 6 best life lessons we learned from our first jobs. (2019). Retrieved from https://www.theladders.com/career-advice/6-best-life-lessons-we-learned-from-our-first-jobs

5. 6 best life lessons we learned from our first jobs. (2019). Retrieved from https://www.theladders.com/career-advice/6-best-life-lessons-we-learned-from-our-first-jobs

6. Experts on the Future of Work, Jobs Training and Skills. (2019). Retrieved from https://www.pewresearch.org/internet/2017/05/03/the-future-of-jobs-and-jobs-training/

7. How to nail the question, "What did you learn in your last job?". (2019). Retrieved 26 December 2019, from https://www.fastcompany.com/40576838/how-to-nail-the-question-what-did-you-learn-in-your-last-job

8. 11 Key Skills You Can Gain from Work Experience. (2019). Retrieved from https://www.careeraddict.com/work-experience-skills

9. 5 Ways to Motivate Yourself to Action. (2019). Retrieved from https://www.dumblittleman.com/5-ways-to-motivate-yourself-to-action/

10. Green Business Trends and What to Expect | Smart Cities Dive. (2020). Retrieved from https://www.smartcitiesdive.com/ex/sustainablecitiescollective/green-business-trends-and-what-expect/1182102/

11. What the Future of Green Technology looks like - Soulful Concepts. (2020). Retrieved from https://soulfulconcepts.com/index.php/2017/05/05/the-future-of-green-technology/

12. 18 Ways to Motivate Yourself. (2020). Retrieved from https://greatist.com/grow/motivation-tips-that-work

13. How Future Technology Impacts Employees | Clutch.co. (2018). Retrieved from https://clutch.co/hr/resources/how-future-technology-impacts-employees

14. McClelland, C. (2018). The Impact of Artificial Intelligence - Widespread Job Losses. Retrieved from

https://www.iotforall.com/impact-of-artificial-intelligence-job-losses/

15. Kids, P. (2016). Why Is STEM Education So Important? Retrieved from https://www.engineeringforkids.com/about/news/2016/february/why-is-stem-education-so-important-/

16. Artificial Intelligence Technology | Top 18 Technologies Used in AI. (2019). Retrieved from https://www.educba.com/artificial-intelligence-technology/

17. Emerging Technologies. (2018). Retrieved from https://www.em-t.com/

18. 2011-2020, (. (2019). Effective Team-Working | SkillsYouNeed. Retrieved from https://www.skillsyouneed.com/ips/team-working.html

19. Garner, J. (2018). Surround yourself with success and like-minded people. Retrieved from https://www.linkedin.com/pulse/surro

und-yourself-success-like-minded-people-janine-garner

20. Bokhari, D. (2019). Action Leads to Motivation (not the other way around). Retrieved from https://www.deanbokhari.com/acton-leads-motivation/

21. Harari, Y. (2018). *Homo Deus : A Brief History Of Tomorrow*. Harpercollins.

22. LEE, K. (2019). *AI SUPERPOWERS*. [S.l.]: MARINER BOOKS.

23. Bolles, R. *What color is your parachute? 2017.*

24. Steve Nguyen, P., Steve Nguyen, P., & Steve Nguyen, P. (2020). Workplace Psychology. Retrieved 7 January 2020, from https://workplacepsychology.net/

25. Acemoglu, D., & Restrepo, P. (2017). Robots and Jobs: Evidence from US Labor Markets. *SSRN Electronic Journal*. DOI: 10.2139/ssrn.2940245

26. Helpman, E. (2019). General Purpose Technologies and Economic Growth. Retrieved from https://mitpress.mit.edu/books/general-purpose-technologies-and-economic-growth

CPSIA information can be obtained
at www.ICGtesting.com
Printed in the USA
LVHW111731060520
655123LV00001B/66

9 781916 355026